HERE COMES BABY!

The Survival Guide for the
Transition to Parenthood

Best Wishes —

Michelle

Praise for "HERE COMES BABY!"

"Here Comes Baby!" is a highly readable and useful guide! In a frank, but humorous way, it details both the joys and realities of having a baby. It is a practical resource for first-time parents filled with helpful options and indispensable survival techniques for the exciting adventure of parenting!"

Stephen L. Abbott, M.D.
Children's Medical Clinic of Santa Barbara

"At last! A reference book on parenting with a personal touch. *Here Comes Baby!* is an invaluable source of information and emotional support for new parents."

Cheryl Siebert, R.N.
Mother of two

"*Here Comes Baby!* embraces and celebrates the magical adventure of parenthood. It is a valuable resource that not only addresses the adjustment of having a baby, but unlike others, provides insight into marital and personal changes as well. It really gives you a "heads up" on the whole "event" of parenting."

Allison Heiduk,
Elementary School Educator
Mother of twins

"*Here Comes Baby!* enriches your own postpartum experience because of Michelle's open and honest discussion about postpartum depression. Thank you, Michelle!"

Jane Honikman
Founder, Postpartum Support International

"I think readers will benefit from Michelle's personal touch, especially concerning communication between partners, and forming a vision for the young family. Candidates for postpartum depression can take comfort and encouragement from her story—they are not alone. Well done, Michelle!"

Allan Kroeker
Film Director and Father of two

"Early parenting put purely and simply. A resource for those inside and outside the (*Medical*) field from undergraduate to Ph.D."

Berne B. Bahnson M.D.
Neurologist/Psychiatrist

"It used to be that families had a grandmother or aunt to offer advice and ease the transition to parenthood. Today, we rely on books by experts. Books like this convey a valuable message, educate and make ours a better world."

Dan Poynter
Author, Publisher and Speaker

"*Here Comes Baby!* teaches you what quality childcare looks like."

Marilynn Jorgensen,
Director of Discoveries Pre-school and
Toddler Center

"*Here Comes Baby!* is sure to offer support and encouragement to first-time parents. Having been witness to the suffering and joy of Michelle's arduous second pregnancy, I can assure readers that their story is a true celebration of family, faith and commitment to parenting."

Dr. Dale Lindsay Morgan
Pastor and Mother

". . . I've been engrossed this book. Believe me when I say there are other things I should be doing [now] but I just couldn't quit reading! Michelle's insights into the wonderful and terrifying experience of becoming a Mother are heartfelt and constructive. Not only does she share her experience, but she is candidly honest and vulnerable. Her practical suggestions are authentic, able to breathe relief and relaxation into a new Mom. A valuable and handy resource!"

Lawanna Busby St. Clair
Speaker, Author and Mother

"*Here Comes Baby!* is an easy to read, entertaining and highly informative reference. I consider it an essential guide for anyone embarking on the parenting journey!"

Dr. Monika McCoy
Chiropractor

HERE COMES BABY!
THE SURVIVAL GUIDE FOR THE TRANSITION TO PARENTHOOD

Michelle S. Brenner

The Samuel Paige Group

Published by:
The Samuel Paige Group
Santa Barbara, California, U.S.A.

Publisher's Cataloging-in-Publication

(Provided by Quality Books, Inc.)

Brenner, Michelle S.
    Here comes baby! : the survival guide for the transition to
parenthood / Michelle S. Brenner. — 1st ed.
    p. cm.
    Includes bibliographical references.
    ISBN: 0-9707654-2-8

    1. Parenting. 2. Pregnancy. 3. Infants—Care. 4. Child rearing.
5. Parenthood. I. Title.

HQ755.8.B74 2001   649'.10242
                                         QBI01-200103

Editing: *Gail M. Kearns, GMK Editorial & Writing Services, Santa Barbara, CA*

Copyediting: *Barbara Coster, Cross-t.i Copyediting, Santa Barbara, CA*

Cover and Book Layout Conception: *Kristi S. Golden, Sioux Falls, SD*

Cover Photo: *L.J. Photography, Santa Barbara, CA*

Cover Design: *Peri Poloni, Knockout Design, Cameron Park, CA*

Design and Typography: *Christine Nolt, Cirrus Design, Santa Barbara, CA*

Printed in the United States of America

CONTENTS

To my two fabulous children
You've brought joy and fulfillment to my life in ways
I never dreamed possible and magnificent chaos
I never imagined. I love you, Sugarbears!

To my husband
I'm so glad you encouraged me to take this incredible
journey called parenthood.

Thank you for being my partner, companion, and the
love of my life, but most of all for loving me just the way I am.
Without your support, this book would never have happened.

To my parents
Thank you for daring to be parents, and especially for being mine.
You've always been there to make a difference when it
counted most. I've always loved you;
now I truly appreciate you.

I love you more than the raven loves his treasure,
More than the dog loves his tail,
More than the whale loves his spout.

Barbara M. Joosse
Mama, Do You Love Me?

Introduction

The mere fact that you're reading this tells me that you, or someone you love, is having or thinking about having a baby. Congratulations! Having a baby is one of the most amazing adventures in life.

My husband and I weren't exactly in a hurry when it came to having children. It took us seven years of marriage to decide to take the plunge. We were on a cruise in Alaska when we learned I was pregnant. We were elated, of course, but at the same time I could feel the panic creeping up the back of my neck. I had owned and managed a small group of hair salons for ten years, but I had serious doubts that I could manage caring for a newborn baby.

As soon as we returned home from our trip, I began to search for a simple, yet comprehensive list of what I needed to get and do, to be ready for the arrival of our first child. I scoured baby stores and bookstores to no avail. Granted, I found many fine books written on the complete birthing experience and even more on various philosophies of child rearing. What I couldn't locate was a practical guide for preparing one's heart and home for bringing a baby into our world.

Here Comes Baby! was written to provide guidance for the path from pregnancy to parenthood. My desire is to prepare new parents for the multiple challenges they face in the first three months after the baby arrives home. All partners face changes in their interpersonal relationship when they add and infant to their world. At the same time, both partners are attempting to acquire parenting skills, manage changes in their personal freedoms and adapt to new life routines. No wonder new parents often feel overwhelmed!

If you're a single parent, it's important to build a support system early on with perhaps your family or close friends.

In a candid, lighthearted manner, this book will make it possible for you and your partner to savor this magical time in your life. *Here Comes Baby!* combines important tips, how-to information, personal stories of pregnancy and parenthood, essential forms and lists, and an extensive appendix of resources for those embarking on their own parenting expedition. Together with Dr. Carole Buchholz and I, and the gracious contributions of several mothers of young children, you can proceed on your parenting adventure confidently, equipped with the combined wisdom and experience of many other parents.

You'll notice in this book that babies are usually referred to as "she" or "her." This is for the sake of simplicity. Please feel free to insert your own preference as you like.

The Expedition Begins

Chapter 1

The Expedition Begins

It's a funny thing about babies—babies of any kind. Whether they come with fingers and toes, paws, feathers, or fur, they all have an irresistible magnetism. I suppose their innate irresistibility is part of the grand plan for the survival of the species. But I believe there's more to it. There's something mystical and magical about birth; it reminds us that we're all part of something larger than ourselves.

Now it's your turn to take your place in the great circle of life. I love what Bill Cosby says in his book *Fatherhood*: "Yes, having a child is surely the most irrational act two people in love can commit." So, welcome to the land of lunacy. Now that you've decided to trade in your quiet evenings, intimate dinners, and weekend rendezvous to venture out into uncharted territory, don't worry, I'm here to help you get your bearings.

CHOOSING THE PARENTING LIFE

I'll bet you hardly realized that the journey into parenthood actually began when you chose your mate. It happens at different times and in different ways for everyone. But sooner or later, when you get serious about a partner, you ask, "Would I want this person to be the father or mother of my children?" And so it begins. Typically, the next big step toward parenthood is when one of you asks the other how they feel about having children.

3

SO, DO WE WANT TO HAVE KIDS . . . !?

The big question is: Do you want to have children? A couple might discuss having children several times over the course of their relationship. Soon after they start dating, many couples make their desires known about whether to have or not to have children. Some people make wonderful companions and lovers but may not be interested in being parents. As a rule, a degree of compatibility in this area is necessary before a serious relationship develops.

As a couple gets closer to tying the knot, there will undoubtedly be more conversations about starting a family—when to begin having kids and how many are the basics. Unfortunately, at the point in a relationship when couples contemplate marriage, they tend to focus mainly on their similarities and ignore their differences. This can present problems later on if their expectations, in fact, turn out to be extremely different. If you've ever seen the "getting engaged" scene in the Woody Allen film Everyone Says I Love You, you know what I'm talking about. If you haven't seen it, let me share it with you. Holden (played by Edward Norton) is telling Shyler (played by Drew Barrymore) how he foresees things once they're married. It goes something like this:

Holden:	When we get married and we live near my parents in Sharon—
Shyler:	Oh, I could never leave New York.
Holden:	Right, we live in New York, of course, but at some point we may want a little more space if we have four kids.
Shyler:	I want two children.
Holden:	Two kids— two is perfect for me, 'cause you know four is really a lot, and you'll be able to stay home with them—
Shyler:	No, I'll be working.

| Holden: | I mean when you're not working full-time—Of course you're going to have a full career in journalism. |
| Shyler: | Architecture. |

Talk about communicating! By the end of this scene, you wonder if these two know anything about each other. But the point is well made. Get to know all you can about each other's likes and dislikes before entering the parent zone. Do you like to spend your evenings out on the town, or are you content to spend a few evenings at home? Do you and your partner feel comfortable sharing domestic chores like laundry and grocery shopping? How many siblings does each of you have? Would you like to have a family of a similar size as the one you grew up in? These are the kinds of questions to ask yourself and each other to see if the parenting lifestyle is really for you.

In our case, my husband, Mark, and I agreed that we wanted to wait at least two or three years before we even considered starting a family. As I mentioned earlier, it turned out to be much longer than that.

MARK'S PROPOSAL

Today we hear a lot about "commitment phobia," specifically with regard to marriage. In retrospect, it wasn't marriage that had frightened Mark or me, it was the "B" word—BABY—that terrified us. We were living an ideal professional life filled with travel, personal gratification and work we found rewarding. We reaped the benefits of our hard work, enjoying a thoroughly comfortable way of life. I used to describe us as classic DINKS (Dual Income No Kids). After more than five years of marriage, my family had begun to think that we would not be adding children to our life.

One summer I had an especially busy travel schedule. One day, Mark voiced his unhappiness about my being on the road so much.. I thought it was a bit strange, since we were both happy in our careers and with each other. I suggested we talk about it when I got back.

I returned home to Santa Barbara on a gorgeous evening and Mark took me to the pier for dinner. As we were enjoying the gentle sea breeze and getting caught up on the events of the past week, out popped the question. Mark wanted to know if I would be interested in having a baby. There it was—after all these years, Mark had decided he wanted to become a dad.

TRAILBLAZING INTO PARENTHOOD

Marriage is most definitely a commitment, and becoming parents is yet another level of commitment. It's important for each partner to take a look at his or her own family background to identify the styles and philosophies of child rearing that they experienced in their respective homes. Consciously or not, all new parents bring elements from their own childhood into the parenting experience. Each partner embodies the possibilities and perplexities of their own family experience, which in turn influence their own ideas about how children should be raised.

Ideally, any couple contemplating having kids should try baby-sitting together a few times so they see what being around small children is really about. Don't get me wrong—I'm not suggesting you give up all of the romantic, candlelight dinners you've been having since your honeymoon. But getting some experience with small children is a good reality check. I'm sure you know someone with kids who would be delighted to have you lend a hand for an evening so they can indulge themselves in one of those long lost candlelight dinners.

TEAMMATES IN PARENTING

The best time for you and your partner to begin thinking of yourselves as parenting teammates is immediately after the astonishment of finding out you're pregnant fades and reality sets in. The more involved you and your partner are in the pregnancy from the beginning, the better off your parenting partnership will be once the baby arrives. All too often, the dad-to-be becomes a spectator and feels left out of the pregnancy as the mother-to-be becomes preoccupied with the baby and frequently turns to women friends and family for emotional support. It's essential to maintain open channels of communication about all aspects of what's happening with the pregnancy and your relationship. There are sure to be highs and lows, and it's so important not to assume that your partner knows what you're thinking or feeling.

In addition to all the excitement that comes with expecting a baby, probably some fears and concerns will also surface. Often, a woman's primary focus is on her body—staying healthy, eating well, exercising appropriately, and preparing a place in the home for the baby. In her partner's case, he may feel stressed by the additional financial responsibility of adding a baby to the family or be anxious about his role in the labor and delivery, as well as caring for a newborn. You both may have reservations about limiting your personal and social time once the baby arrives. (These reservations are valid, because inevitably, changes will occur in this area.) For better or worse, with the arrival of your first child, your lives will be filled with new and unfamiliar activities. All relationships will require more flexibility and patience as you adjust to life with a newborn.

As you might also expect, sex may become an issue during pregnancy and the postpartum period. Hormonal changes can dramatically increase or inhibit the sex drive for some women during this time. Individual responses to pregnancy and parenthood are as unique as each person. Some women describe being pregnant as the sexiest time in their lives. For others, it can be the most upsetting-both physically and emotionally. Most, however, fall somewhere in between.

As for men, some find their pregnant partners absolutely irresistible, while others are inhibited by the physical changes of their partner during pregnancy. In extreme cases, some men are hesitant to have sex during pregnancy out of fear that intercourse might in some way injure the fetus. This is highly unlikely.

This is just a small sampling of the issues and areas of concern that may arise during pregnancy. As I said before, talking candidly and sensitively about your needs and new feelings with your spouse is crucial to the growth of the partnership.

GETTING TO THE FUN STUFF

In addition to the more serious aspects of becoming a family, there are lots of fun things to do at this point. My husband and I thoroughly enjoyed tracking our pregnancy with a special calendar where we read about our baby's development each week. Reading *What to Expect When You're Expecting* by Arlene Eisenberg, et al., became a nightly ritual and one that I highly recommend. Another fun activity is choosing colors and accessories for the nursery. Dad may not want to admit it, but secretly he may have his own preferences about the nursery. Encourage him to get involved from the start.

NAMING THE NEXT GENERATION

Beginning the search for your baby's name is one of the most fun things you can do with your partner. Mark and I had many wonderful evenings working and laughing our way through stacks of baby name books. As we perused the pages of names and the stories about their meanings, we tried out hundreds of possibilities—some more ridiculous than others.

In the beginning, write down any and every name that strikes your fancy. There will be plenty of time and input from others about which ones to delete. However, don't let others unduly influence your decision. In short, I encourage you to do plenty of lighthearted surveying before you get serious about selecting your nominees.

Some other places to look for names in addition to books include your newspaper and hall of public records. Our local paper publishes a monthly list of all the babies born the previous month. Checking this list serves two purposes: it's a resource for baby names and combinations as well as a barometer of current naming trends. It'll also give you an indication of what names you can expect your children's classmates to have in the future. This may or may not be of concern to you. If it is, you can take it one step further and consult your county clerk.

Other things to consider when naming your baby: How does it sound with your last name? Is it easy to pronounce and spell? What nicknames could be associated with the name? What will the initials look like together—do they spell out an odd or unappealing word? Is it a name you'd like to have yourself?

> My father's name is Gordon Albert Stewart. While he and my mother were still dating, my mother bought him a gift of cologne and was having it monogrammed. The clerk asked for the name, "Gordon Stewart," she replied. "Is there a middle initial, miss", the clerk continued. "Yes, it's Albert." A few moments later the clerk began to chuckle. My mother was a bit offended until the clerk turned the flask around. The initials read "G.A.S."

I find that some parents want a unique name, while others simply want the name they want. Other couples have a family name they intend to use, or they want a name that reflects their ethnic or religious background. I'll say it again: Be sure to choose a name that both you and your partner like, because you'll be hearing it and saying it for the next forty or fifty years.

Selecting a name too far in advance can create a dilemma. What if you've got your heart set on a name that simply doesn't match your baby's personality? If you have other friends and acquaintances who are expecting and they deliver first and choose the same name, will you still be comfortable using it? The name you've loved since the eleventh grade may currently be the most common name in the country—will that make a difference?

With all this said, be aware that if you choose a name that doesn't work a few weeks or months into your baby's life, you can change the name. If you intend to change the first name, try to do so within the first three to six months after your baby's birth. Middle names are far less time sensitive and can be changed at virtually any point in one's life.

WHAT DO YOU MEAN IT'S A GIRL!

My husband comes from a family that has had only boy babies on his father's side for the last four generations. Since the male genetics determine the baby's sex, when we got around to selecting names, our most serious considerations were for boy names. Our favorite was Mason Stewart.

Although we chose not to find out the sex of our baby until it arrived, I spent the last few months of my pregnancy looking at boy things, mulling over combinations of boy names, and mentally preparing for a baby boy. But I picked out a rather gender-neutral Southwest crib set just in case our bouncing baby boy surprised us.

When I went into pre-term labor and there was serious concern that our baby was coming two months early, my husband showed up at the hospital with all our baby name books and reminded me that we didn't have a girl's name. " Just in case," he said. Fortunately, the pre-term labor was stopped and we did go full term. And we now had some ideas for naming a baby girl, though I didn't think we'd need it. The big day arrived and the doctor announced proudly, "It's a girl!" My response, "Are you sure?," didn't make him take another look. So our Mason Stewart quickly became Paige Meredith Brenner.

SUMMARY

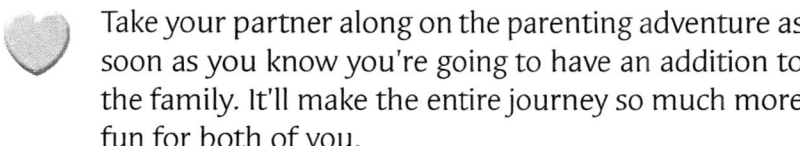 Take your partner along on the parenting adventure as soon as you know you're going to have an addition to the family. It'll make the entire journey so much more fun for both of you.

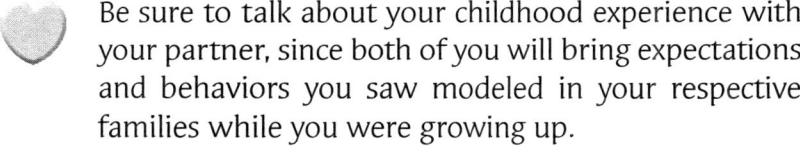 Be sure to talk about your childhood experience with your partner, since both of you will bring expectations and behaviors you saw modeled in your respective families while you were growing up.

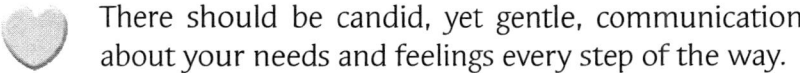 There should be candid, yet gentle, communication about your needs and feelings every step of the way.

Choosing your baby's name is fun. Begin thinking about names for your baby early on. Try not to let too many outsiders influence your final decision.

Naming the Next Generation

Brainstorming

Contenders

Favorites for Boys

Favorites for Girls

The Winners!

Financing the Expedition

Chapter 2

Financing the Expedition

Starting a family isn't just an event, it's a lifestyle that requires planning and patience throughout. Raising a child is an expensive proposition, one that costs plenty of money in the short term and the long run. This begins with buying the nursery furnishings and ongoing supplies for your newborn, providing for your child's education, and well beyond.

I can't overemphasize the importance of staying within your financial means each step of the way. What could be worse than going into debt in the very beginning of your adventure and consequently limiting your family's future? Medical expenses and baby gear are only the beginning—so sharpen your pencil and get out your note pad and calculator—here we go!

FINANCIAL REALITY STRIKES

The medical costs for a normal, healthy pregnancy, including prenatal care and delivery, may range from $3,000 to $6,500. A more complicated pregnancy can run upwards of $15,000. This doesn't include sick baby care if your baby experiences any complications. A newborn intensive care unit (ICU) runs approximately $2,500 per day. Costs vary greatly from region to region and from one insurance program to another. One thing is certain: being uninsured is the most expensive way to have a baby. Not only will you pay all the charges yourself, but you will not have the benefit of contracted price limits on services, so your charges will be at the maximum rate.

It can realistically cost four times as much for the services involved with pregnancy and delivery if you're uninsured and paying cash. So if you're reading this book in preparation for having a family, get insured or stay insured before getting pregnant. Once you're pregnant, you're uninsurable for pregnancy under an individual policy. Some good news for this situation is that more and more states are providing insurance programs for expectant women. California and Washington are leading the way in this area. If you have questions or would like more information, check with your state Department of Insurance to learn about benefits you may be eligible for. Clearly, having a baby is a time when insurance is a significant benefit.

> *Katherine is a single woman, self-employed, working in sales—and also self-insured. When renewing her insurance policy for another year, she decided to save some money on her premiums and drop the maternity coverage. Recently divorced and not planning to have a baby, she was astonished when, much to her dismay, her birth control failed and she became pregnant. Since her pregnancy wasn't covered by her insurance, her attempt to save money on the premiums turned out to be shortsighted and put her under significant financial strain and emotional stress.*

If a mother-to-be is employed and insured through her employer, in most cases, she's better off financially using her employer's insurance program. If you're insured through your spouse or on a family plan, your premiums and deductibles may be higher. If your doctor isn't in your insurance company's network, payouts will be made at a lower rate.

Unless instructed otherwise, a newborn is added to the mother's policy, not the father's. This becomes significant if the mother chooses not to go back to work. If that's in question, add the baby to the father's insurance policy. You must call whichever insurance company you want to use and notify them of your baby's arrival within thirty days. With most insurance companies, all you do is call the customer service number and tell them the baby's name and date of birth. Failure to do this within the specified time limit of your policy can have drastic results such as loss of benefits or complete loss of coverage for your infant. The bottom line here is that it's definitely worth your effort to be informed about the maternity coverage provided through each partner's insurance policy.

If you've already had some experience working with your insurance company, you're one step ahead of the game. Knowing how to submit your claims and insurance requests in insurance industry language will help expedite payments and save you time and money.

INSURANCE

BASIC INSURANCE INFORMATION GUIDE

Each of your health care providers throughout your pregnancy, delivery, postnatal, and new baby care will need certain information from you. If you have an insurance card, bring it with you for each appointment. It generally has the information on it that you'll need.

Basic Information

Member's name:
Social security number:
Employer's name:
Policy number:
Effective dates:
Co-pay amounts:
Deductibles and Co-Pays
Family deductible:

Individual deductible:

Mother's deductible:

Baby's deductible:

> (Note: If your policy's calendar year changes before delivery, find out how charges and deductibles will be handled.)

Percentage of your payout: (10%/90%, 20%/80%, 30%/70%)

Co-pay per visit: (Typically $5 to $25 per visit)

Maximum out-of-pocket expense cap:

Additional Information

Account number:

Plan code:

Benefits code:

Telephone information number:

Mailing address:

Questions and Policy Information

As you evaluate your policy, the following coverage issues should be analyzed.

- Does the policy allow you to select your own physician and hospital, or are you required to use those specified by the insurance policy's network of providers?

- Does your physician of choice have admitting privileges to your hospital of choice?

- How does the policy handle preexisting conditions?

- Does the insurance company need to be notified about the pregnancy and estimated due date?

- Is preapproval required for tests, procedures, or medications? If so, what items require preapproval and how is this done?

- How many days/hours in the hospital does your policy cover for post-   delivery? Under what conditions?

- Does the policy have a "reasonable and customary" clause? (This means the policy pays what is considered average for your area, which may be lower than what you've actually been billed. In some cases, your health care provider may waive the difference, so be sure you know the situation.)

- Who is responsible for handling the documentation? Who submits the claims to the insurance company— you, your health care provider, or your employer?

- How will your payments be made? Will the insurance company pay the providers directly, or do you pay the bills and then get reimbursed?

- When can the baby be added to the policy? Requirements regarding this vary from company to company. Be sure you know. Otherwise, you could be penalized with a reduction in coverage or no coverage at all.

- It's a good idea to document how, when, and by whom your insurance questions were answered. Keep all bills and receipts—doctor, pharmacy, prescriptions, etc.—in a file folder. Retain photocopies of everything you submit to the insurance company. It's amazing how many things go wrong in a paper chase. Maintaining good records will save you money in the end.

- If you have questions regarding any aspect of your maternity coverage, call your insurance company's customer service number. They have the specifics about your coverage.

DISABILITY AND LIFE INSURANCE

Disability and life insurance are never more important than when you decide to have children. As a rule, healthy adults can find a way to support themselves that will provide for their basic needs. Children and babies cannot. It's only reasonable that a parent would make every effort to provide for their offspring in the event they can no longer fulfill their responsibilities to their child. Insurance coverage is one way to do this and should begin long before baby arrives.

We've all heard heart-wrenching stories of a young couple who are expecting a baby and the husband is suddenly taken ill or has a fatal accident before the baby's birth. As tragic as the death of a parent is, whether before birth or in the early years of a child's life, a severely disabling accident or illness can leave a family in greater financial distress than when death occurs. In addition to the emotional strain, the financial realities of long-term medical care and loss of income can be staggering. This is why I take the position that disability and life insurance are essential.

Did you know:

- Between the ages of thirty-five and sixty-five, seven out of ten people will become disabled for three months or longer.*

- One out of seven employees will be disabled for five years or more before retirement.*

- At age thirty-two, a disability of three months or longer is six times more likely than death.*

- In recent years, seven out of ten claims for Social Security disability benefits were initially refused.**

[* Commissioner's Disability Table ** Senate Finance Committee]

Unless you're financially independent and don't have to work, everyone who uses their current income to maintain their lifestyle should seriously consider disability insurance. Many companies offer disability insurance to their employees. If they don't, you can obtain your own individual coverage. Although good medical insurance can protect you from bankruptcy in the case of a large medical claim, it will not take care of your mortgage, food, utilities, and other living expenses required for a family.

I strongly suggest that you review any disability insurance that may be available through your employer or your partner's employer. If there is no program available to you through work, investigate private insurance companies in your area. At the same time that you're exploring disability insurance, look at their life insurance programs.

Life insurance can be used to pay off your mortgage, outstanding debts, and education tuition or to help supplement income. The general rule of thumb for how much life insurance to have is approximately six times your annual income. If you decide that you want to have life insurance, check with an insurance company in your area who will evaluate your individual needs.

In addition to the insurance, it's in your family's best interest to have current wills and an estate plan, regardless of the size and amount of your assets. A trust will save a significant percentage of your assets from being taken away in taxes, as well as a tremendous amount of stress and strain on your partner. In a worst case scenario, if neither you nor your partner is legally competent, be sure the will and trust spell out how and by whom you wish your child to be cared for.

This information about insurance and estate planning is a general overview at best. Insurance and estate laws are regulated by each individual state. Consequently, you must get help from a professional who knows the laws and regulations of your state of residence. It's well worth your time and effort. Most people assume they can put this off until they're older. Don't do it. Make the necessary arrangements based on your current status and amend them as time and life changes require.

ROUTINE EXPENSES WITH A NEW BABY

Basic items like formula, diapers, wipes, and Tylenol are recurring expenses. I advise that you stay with your doctor's recommendations and brand names for items like formula and acetaminophen. As for items like diapers and wipes, use whatever works best for you and your baby and gives you the best value for your budget. Watch for sales and use coupons whenever possible.

Formula is essential to your baby's health. This isn't the place to try to save money by substituting with anything other than what your doctor recommends. Many new parents are tempted to stock up on formula in advance of the baby's arrival. Don't do it! You can't predict which formula will be best for your infant's delicate system. If you bottle-feed, you'll most likely want to use the formula the baby is given in the hospital nursery, at least initially. If you plan to nurse, you won't be using formula for several months.

In addition to the medical expenses traditionally covered by insurance, you'll incur other predictable expenses. The following is an overview of the most common items and their approximate costs:

ONGOING SUPPLIES AND EXPENSES

Item	Amount Used	Price	Type
Diapers	8-12 per day	$6-8	24 per pkg
		$13-15	48 per pkg
Formula	24-32 oz per day	$3-5 qt	Ready-to-feed
		$3-5 qt.	Concentrate
		$5-6 qt	Special
		$7-11 14 oz	Powder
		$21 & up/ 2 lbs.	Powder

Baby wipes	$3-4	80 count
Barrier cream	$3-4	3 oz
	$12-15	1 lb
Liquid acetaminophen	$5-6 1.5 oz	Tylenol brand
	$3-4 1.5 oz	Generic
Film and processing	$11-16	35 mm

MONEY-SAVING TIPS

- Shop with a list and stick to it.

- Buy items on sale when available.

- Use coupons.

- Avoid shopping at convenience stores, because prices tend to be higher for small quantities.

- Join your supermarket's shopping club if it has one. If it doesn't, think about choosing a market that does.

- Powder formula is more economical than other types. Limit your use of concentrate and ready-to-feed formulas to those times when traveling and other special occasions.

- Avoid purchasing supplies in "gift" packaging, since the per item cost tends to be much higher.

THE COST OF CHILD CARE

I'm finding that many women are ambivalent about whether or not to return to work after their newborn arrives. This decision is a uniquely individual and most personal choice. In addition to the emotional issues, be keenly aware that child care is a significant expense, particularly newborn infant care, one for which a game plan and a budget is needed.

As you begin investigating child care and its costs, take into account the fact that some women have found they're financially ahead by staying home with their new baby. When you compare the routine costs involved with working, child care, professional clothing, and transportation costs, you may be surprised to find how little of your income is left. If you have insurance or other benefits through your employment, be sure to consider these as part of the whole compensation and cost comparison.

If you do plan to return to work, compare the total costs of in-home child care with infant day care facilities available in your area. For more information, see Exploring Child Care in the "Setting Up Camp" chapter of this book.

THE PRICE YOU PAY

The cost and availability of child care varies from region to region. Generally, one-on-one care is more expensive than group day care. The rate for hiring an individual caregiver ranges from $6 to $12+ per hour. Credentials and experience greatly influence the hourly rate of a nanny or other professionally trained caregivers. Group day care, whether in a home or center, starts at about $3 per hour but doesn't usually exceed $7 per hour. When it does, group care begins to cost as much as one-on-one and prices itself out of the market. It's important to remember that price doesn't necessarily determine the quality of care.

If you pay a baby-sitter or other type of child care provider more than $1,100 a year, the IRS requires you to deduct Social Security taxes. You'll need to get your caregiver's Social Security number and file the appropriate tax forms. Call or visit your local IRS office to pick up Publication 926, Household Employer's Tax Guide or download it off the Internet at the IRS Web site: www.irs.ustreas.gov ("Forms & Pubs"). This will help you determine what your tax responsibilities are. NOTE: Laws differ from year to year and state to state, so it's vital that you get current

IRS information, whether it's through your accountant or on your own.

Some employers have benefit plans that allow you to deduct pretax dollars from your income to help cover your dependent care expenses. Check both your own benefit package and your partner's to see what they provide with regard to child care.

SUMMARY

Keeping money matters in order and maintaining financial health is essential to your family's long-term success and happiness. Often the biggest struggle a family faces is over money concerns. If you and your partner have not put much thought or discussion into your family's financial future, now is an excellent time to do so. If you need some help, check the appendix for some good reading material or ask your banker or financial planning consultant to schedule a budgeting consultation with you. Consider where you can economize. Then talk candidly about your optional spending habits and how you can cut down on those expenditures.

 Whatever you choose to do about your employment status, be absolutely sure you have health insurance coverage through an employer or independent coverage.

 If insurance premiums are an issue, with a little research you can find a preferred provider program (PPO) or health maintenance organization (HMO) in your area that will accommodate your financial circumstances.

 Keep in mind that price is not the ultimate test of quality when it comes to child care.

Take the time to thoroughly investigate the child care options in your area. You'll probably be able find satisfactory arrangements at a price that fits your budget.

 Sharpen your bargain-hunting skills. You'll be amazed how much more you can get for your money with a little extra effort and creativity.

Selecting Your Gear

Chapter 3

Selecting Your Gear

GEARING UP

The amount of paraphernalia required for the care and feeding of a tiny newborn is amazing! Acquiring all the "stuff" adds up quickly in terms of dollars, especially in the beginning. There are many places to get the items you need and want: baby boutiques, department stores, mail order catalogs, on-line shopping, nearly new or used clothing stores, and borrowing from family and friends.

Before you go on a shopping spree, first, think about which things could prove to have sentimental value and which are simply everyday necessities. Although they weren't expensive, the outfits my children came home from the hospital in were soft and cozy, and I've saved them both as mementos. Second, take a look at my Essential Gear shopping list that follows. This will help you decide how much of your budget you want to spend on which articles. It will also help you decide where you want to shop.

If you take these two steps, I can assure you you'll get the maximum value from your budget, save precious time and energy, and keep the shopping fun. The easiest way to start is by using the telephone. Start with the phone book, call the stores in your area, and ask what they carry in the way of furnishings, clothing, and/or accessories. If you have the time and inclination, start doing some window-shopping well in advance of your delivery date to get a feel for what's available. Most of all, have a great time doing it and take your partner along now and then!

UNPREPARED!

It was a cold, dark morning in mid-December when I found myself being admitted to the hospital labor and delivery ward two months earlier than expected. We were stunned by the prospect of our baby's premature arrival. At that moment, our anticipated nursery was an office/guest room and our crib was standing unassembled in the garage. We were totally unprepared!

Fortunately, the pre-term labor was stabilized, and when the shock faded, we began to think about what to do next. We didn't have any of the provisions necessary to bring a baby home—not even a bag of diapers! Fortunately for us, a dear friend and mother of two came to our rescue. She quickly scribbled a list of essentials on a scrap of paper and handed it to my husband. Now he was a man with a mission. This dad-to-be was off to the baby store to get the items our friend said we would need to care for our newborn. Later that day, he arrived home with the fruits of his labor: a dresser, rocking chair, infant baby tub, and other items too abundant to mention.

Our baby daughter was born in February. Thanks to friends and family, we were able to collect all the essential gear we needed. Paige arrived home happy, healthy and full-term to a full nursery.

WHAT TO BUY

In the beginning, babies eat, sleep, and fill diapers—with some gurgling and crying mixed in. The Essential Gear list contains the things you need most in the first eight to twelve weeks. My list begins with an infant car seat, since most hospitals won't allow you to take your baby home without one. After this, items are listed in groupings of similar use or function.

When gearing up, there are two kinds of shopping trips. One is for looking—to survey the options—and the other is for buying. Before you buy, make sure you take your shopping list with you! It's too easy to buy items you don't really need and overlook the essentials. The Essential Gear list is a practical, hands-on description of the items and their uses.

ESSENTIAL GEAR

Infant car seat

Bassinet or cradle

Cradle sheets,
    if using small cradle   (2-4)

Crib   (standard size)

Crib mattress

Crib mattress cover,
    waterproof   (1)

Mattress pad   (1-2)

Crib bumper set

Crib sheets   (2-4)

Thermal blankets   (3-5)

Dresser

Changing table

Changing pad & pad covers (2-3)

Diaper pail or covered trashcan

Infant bathtub or sponge mat

Infant first aid kit

Thermometers

Infant nail clippers/scissors

Monitor set

Night-light

Stroller

Diaper bag

Newborn diapers (cloth and
    disposable)

Waterproof pants for cloth diapers
    (2-3)

Safety diaper pins for cloth
    diapers   (3-6 sets)

Disposable
    baby wipes   (1-2 boxes)

Baby bottles   (2-4)

Baby bottle brushes   (1)

Burping towels
    or cloth diapers   (3-8)

Pacifiers   (2-3)

Receiving blankets   (3-6)

Waterproof lap pads   (4-6)

Cotton swabs   (1 box)

Cotton balls or pads   (1 bag)

Rubbing alcohol   (1 bottle)

Barrier cream
    such as Desitin or A&D
        (1 lg. & 1 sm. for
          diaper bag)

Mild shampoo or cleansing lotion
    (1 6-8 oz)

Baby bodysuits ("onesies") (3-6)

Side snap T-shirts   (2-4)

Footed sleepers   (4-6)

Drawstring gowns   (2-3)

Baby caps or bonnets   (2-4)

Socks and booties   (2-4 pairs)

Bibs   (4-6)

Baby wipe warmer

Washcloths   (6-8)

ESSENTIAL GEAR continued

Hooded baby towels	(2-4)	Doughnut head cushion for car seat	
Baby carrier or backpack		Day wear outfits	(3-6)
Car window shade		Crib shoes	(1-2 pairs)
Terry cloth strap covers and head supports for car seat	(2 sets)	Bunting (zip or button)	(1)

OPTIONAL GEAR

Breast pump

Rocking chair with footstool

Camera/video equipment

Radio cassette/CD player

Infant swing

Playpen or port-a-crib

Floor quilt

Infant seat/bouncer seat

Crib mobile

Crib mirror

Crib animal with intrauterine sounds

Music box

Baby toys

Clothes hamper

DESCRIPTION OF GEAR AND HOW TO USE IT

Infant Car Seat

A car seat is an absolute necessity! They're required by law in most states, and most hospitals won't let you take your baby home without one. As a service, many hospitals offer infant car seat rentals in case you don't have one of your own when it's time to leave with your newborn. Car seats come in different sizes and styles and are priced accordingly. Generally, they fit into three categories, depending upon the age and weight of the infant: infant only car seats are for newborns up to twenty pounds; convertibles are for newborns and up to forty pounds; and boosters are for children weighing approximately thirty to sixty pounds.

My husband and I first purchased a convertible type, which we found difficult to use with a newborn. A newborn can't sit fully upright and the seat doesn't fully recline. Newer car seats generally don't have this problem, but be sure to check for this before purchasing. This is particularly important if you're buying a second-hand seat or borrowing an older model. After a week or two of struggling, we purchased an infant only, which also served as a handy portable baby carrier and infant seat when on the move.

ALWAYS FOLLOW THE MANUFACTURER'S INSTRUCTIONS FOR CAR SEAT USE!

There are many other features to consider when buying child restraint seats for auto and air travel. Detachable swivel bases are handy because they allow you turn the infant seat from front to back or side to side without having to remove the base from the automobile's seat belt. The base also allows you to take the seat portion in and out of the car without reattaching the seat belt each time. They do, however, make a loud clicking noise when the seat snaps out of the base, and if you're trying to move a sleeping baby, this can be a negative. You can also secure the automobile's car seat to the car's seat belt without the base. Always follow the manufacturer's instructions that come with the unit.

Twisted handles on an infant car seat make it much easier to carry. The ninety-degree turn in the handle places the hand and arm of the personal carrying it in a more natural, stronger position when transporting the car seat. This is a real plus as the baby gains weight and Mom has to carry the baby and all the other gear at the same time.

Front guards or restraints come in two primary styles: padded armrests (example: Century) or breastplate/tummy guards (example: Fisher-Price). Both styles work, so the best choice may be the one you or your child likes best. Our infants both preferred the breastplate style, which gave them more visibility and a feeling

of openness. Several of our friends' children happily used the
armrest style.

The convertible four-in-one type of car seat/stroller has been
changing and improving and has become quite popular. A major
benefit of this style is that it allows you to transfer the baby from
the car to a stroller without waking the baby. These car seats come
with a frame that the car seat/infant seat snaps into. The car seat
handle moves and can be positioned to use as an infant seat on a
flat surface. The fourth feature allows the frame to be adapted to
a toddler's umbrella-type stroller. This is something to consider
for anyone with back problems because the frame that the seat fits
into is much lighter than a traditional stroller, and you don't have
to lift the frame and the seat at the same time. In some of these
strollers, the baby seat sits quite low. Check out lifting from the
seat of any stroller if back problems are a concern for you.

When your infant grows out of her first car seat, you can take
her with you to a store where you can have her test drive the
various styles of toddler car seats. Notice how she reacts to each
one. I highly recommend that you go when your little one is
rested, well fed, and happy.

If you have any questions concerning car seats for infants, call
the Safe Ride Helpline (800-745-SAFE). It's a wonderful support
service (supported by tax-deductible donations) that is especially
helpful when it comes to recalls on these products. They'll gladly
answer all your questions regarding infant car seats.

Bassinet or Cradle: Newborn to Three Months

Cradles and bassinets come in a variety of styles. They're
especially handy if you live in a multilevel home, since they can
be easily moved from one level to another. Some bassinets have
a romantic, old-fashioned appeal, while others are contempor-
ary in style and have additional features such as wheels.

Many cradles rock from side to side, which is not always a
motion that infants fancy, so if you choose a cradle that rocks, be

sure it also has a stationary setting. If you'll be sleeping in the same room with your newborn, a bassinet or cradle is great for those first few weeks or months. You'll really appreciate having your baby near you for the nighttime feedings. A bassinet-style stroller (with brakes) can serve nicely as a newborn cradle.

Crib

Safety is always first when it comes to buying your full-sized crib. Federal safety regulations have been in effect since 1972. However, even more stringent voluntary standards apply to most cribs designed after 1992. The crib should be sturdy, with slats no more than 2-3/8 inches apart. Consider choosing a crib that has a single-hand drop-side release to make it easier for you to maneuver when you have a sleeping baby in your arms.

When you buy your first crib, keep in mind that you may use it for more than one child. Therefore, I recommend you select a style suitable for either boys or girls. Your baby's crib is one area to avoid hand-me-downs unless it meets current regulations and is sturdy. If you do acquire an older crib, be sure to inspect it for any broken and missing parts. Refinish it with a non-toxic finish, and look for any potential strangling hazards such as corner posts and cutouts on end panels.

Crib Mattress

A crib mattress must fit snugly into the crib. There shouldn't be more than two fingers' width between the mattress and any side of the crib. The firmer the mattress, the better. There is a concern that mattresses that are extremely soft and squishy may increase the risk of SIDS (sudden infant death syndrome)—especially waterbeds. If you have any questions regarding your baby's mattress, consult your pediatrician.

> The American Academy of Pediatrics (AAP)
> strongly recommends against the
> use of waterbeds for infants.

Crib Mattress Cover

A waterproof cover is essential for protecting the mattress from moisture when your baby spits up or overflows a diaper.

Mattress Pad

A fitted mattress pad will add comfort to your child's crib environment. They come in the traditional quilted style, or you can choose from other options such as sheepskin or egg crate foam pads. Check with your pediatrician. Some doctors believe that certain pads have a greater risk of SIDS. Ask which type he or she feels is best for your baby. Follow the manufacturer's instructions on proper use.

Crib Bumper Set

Bumper pads for the crib keep the baby from bumping his or her head against the hard surface of the railings or wedging their head between the slats. Bumper sets come in many colors, patterns, and fabrics, so not only can they protect your baby, they can also liven up the nursery with their decorative possibilities. During the early months, while the baby is small and immobile, rolled towels or blankets can provide the same protection.

Crib Sheets

Even if you place some kind of waterproof protective pads under the baby's bottom, it's a good idea to have two or three fitted sheets on hand as a backup in case the baby's diaper leaks or the baby spits up. To save yourself from having to change the linens often, place a towel and lap pad between your infant and the sheets or buy sheet savers, which are much easier to change than a fitted sheet, especially at 3:00 A.M.

Thermal Blankets

Thermal blankets are lightweight and much more practical than some of the fancy coverlets you'll find on the market. Most have a waffle pattern and provide more warmth and cushioning than the traditional receiving blankets described later on. You should have a few of them on hand. In colder climates, your baby may need more than one blanket for sleeping and going outdoors.

Dresser

A chest of drawers for your baby's clothing and supplies is an item you'll find very hand. A lot depends on how much you buy in the beginning and how many gifts of clothing you receive. Perhaps you have an existing dresser and don't want one that's designed and decorated specifically for young children. In the end, your budget may be the deciding factor. Another approach is to use a few hanging baskets in the closet. If you do plan to invest a significant amount of money in baby furniture, you may want to select a style that works for both boys and girls, especially if you're planning on adding to your family in the future.

Changing Table

There are several types of changing tables. One type is a chest of drawers with a special changing area on the top. Another kind has open shelves under the changing table area. Still others are folding models. You can even purchase a portable changing table with a pad, or just a pad to fit on top of a dresser or counter. All the options have pros and cons with regard to price, mobility, storage, and accessibility.

Consider where your primary changing area will be. Here are some things to consider: Will you need an electrical outlet nearby to plug in a night-light or a warmer for the baby wipes? Will you need extra counter space or a shelf nearby? If you want to have a second changing area, away from the baby's room, a simple, economical changing area can be made by using a bath cushion (described under Infant Bathtub) covered with a hand towel or cloth diaper. This works especially well during the first few months.

Changing Pad and Pad Covers

You'll need a foam pad and two or three washable pad covers for the changing table. Be sure to match up the sizes and styles with your particular changing table and pad. There are several varieties available.

Diaper Pail or Covered Trash Can

This item is a must—even if you can't smell! Whether you choose a Diaper Genie, a Rubbermaid trash can with a lid, or something in between, it's really a personal preference issue. Whatever you choose, the more frequently you empty it, the better off you and your nose will be! Your selection will depend on whether you plan to use disposable or cloth diapers.

Infant Bathtub

Both infant tubs and bath cushions that look like a giant sponge work well. The sponge bath cushion is sculptured to hold the baby more securely, but the choice may depend on where you intend to bathe your infant most often—in the bathtub, bathroom sink, or kitchen sink. The second issue is how much space you have for bathing and storing the tub. The more elaborate tubs take up a significant amount of room. The sponge bath cushion works well in tubs, on counters, or in large sinks and is especially useful for sponge bathing your newborn. The tub works well after the umbilical cord is healed and when the baby is able to sit upright. A tub with a recliner insert for younger babies that can be removed as they get older makes it a much more functional item.

Infant First Aid Kit

Most baby stores and infant departments carry some kind of home infant medical kit. They usually contain a thermometer, nail clippers, safety scissors, ear syringe, nasal aspirator, as well as a few miscellaneous items such as a medicine spoon and medicine dropper.

These items can be purchased individually if kits aren't available or if you only want to purchase specific things. A nose syringe should be used only as a nose aspirator and never placed inside your baby's ear. Always consult your health care professional about your baby's ears. In addition to the items you'll find in a prepackaged kit, I recommend keeping the following products and items on hand to cope with any minor problems that may arise:

Acetaminophen (infant drops and suppositories)

Neosporin ointment

Children's Triaminic cold and cough syrup

Cotton balls and swabs

Alcohol for umbilical cord

Hydrocortisone cream, 1% (small tube)

Plastic adhesive bandages

Saline nose drops

Petroleum jelly

Sunscreen, SPF 15 or 30

Orajel (teething relief medicine)

Cold/hot mist vaporizer for baby's room (inexpensive models work well but may not last as long.

Note: hot mist units must be kept away from infants at all times.

Thermometers

A rectal thermometer is a necessity. They come in both digital and traditional types. The digital ones are slightly more expensive, but they have a quick, easy-to-read display—great for the coward mom who may be panic-stricken the first time she tries to take her infant's temperature. Newborns usually get their temperatures taken rectally or under the arm (not as accurate). Initially, a rectal thermometer is adequate. Recently, I've used a new style, which is a heat-sensing strip that can be pressed against the forehead. It's easy to use, but displays the temperature in ranges of about two degrees, thereby being much less precise than the rectal thermometer.

As your baby grows older and becomes more active, taking his or her temperature rectally is a much more challenging endeavor. At this point, you might consider using the heat strip, a digital underarm style, or an electronic ear thermometer, which displays the temperature in about a second on an illuminated, digital readout. Ear thermometers are designed to be used on children aged one year and older. They're considerably more expensive than other thermometers ($65+) but a nice convenience if your budget allows it. I personally have been delighted with mine now that my children are both over a year old. Do check with your pediatrician about the method he or she prefers.

Ask your health care professional to teach you how to use a rectal thermometer.

Infant Nail Clippers/Scissors

Don't forget this important item. Get the ones that are designed especially for babies. Cutting an infant's fingernails can be a daunting task for a mother, but it's important to do it so your baby doesn't accidentally scratch his or her face. Try accomplishing this chore when your infant is asleep or very relaxed. It worked best for me when my infant was napping or transfixed watching music videos.

Monitor Set

If your living space is larger than a studio or a small one-bedroom apartment, monitor sets are great for peace of mind. It's comforting to be able to hear your baby breathing while you're relaxing (ha, ha!) in another room or taking care of other matters. Most baby equipment manufacturers make monitors, that use either batteries or an AC adapter. Some brands have two listening units, which is useful if you need them in more than one room.

There are some safety concerns to be aware of when using monitors, such as interference with other electronic devices in your home or building and the location of the monitor. Don't place it near a bathtub or other area where it could be immersed in water. Always test the unit for the range or distance in the location where it will be used.

In addition to audio monitors, audiovisual monitors are now available. They're considerably more expensive, though some parents may find them well worth the expense. Please remember that nothing can monitor your baby better than you can, so look upon monitors as merely an aid and check your baby personally on a regular basis.

Night-Light

We have a vast array of night-lights to choose from, from green-glowing, low-energy socket types and small bulb socket lights to decorative lamps of all sizes, shapes, and colors. Night-lights have a soothing effect, which often gives a feeling of security—at any age! They're especially helpful for late-night feeding and changing when you hope to get back to sleep quickly.

Stroller

Some type of stroller is a must. However, selecting the brand and model is a bit like choosing a car. Are you looking for a top-of-the-line luxury model, a light sporty model, or an efficient one at a lower price? Think about how you plan to use your stroller. For example, if you want to jog with your baby every day (more power to you!) then a three-wheel runner's style would be just the ticket. If you need to transport the baby and stroller to other locations regularly, you should consider a lightweight, portable model. Will you and your partner be taking the baby for walks, and will they be more than a block or two? If so, larger wheels tend to be more comfortable for both baby and parent.

Some of the key issues to consider are: the stroller needs to be sturdy, turn well, be easy to collapse and open, and have washable surfaces. (It's best if you can remove the seat covers and wash them.)

As with most of the larger items I suggest, too many features is not always a benefit. Try to identify the features that you'll use and benefit from. Then select a model that has the ones you need and go with your intuition. Features that proved beneficial to me included: maximum sunshade protection, high-quality wheels and brakes, adjustable seat back, sturdy gear/bag holding area, handle leash (extra safety feature), and drink holder. Here's my stroller story.

We were overwhelmed, to say the least, by all the styles and features available in strollers, not to mention price range. We purchased two strollers for our first child. The first was a beautiful, classic-styled carriage, good for long walks. It was sturdy and had large wheels that were great at absorbing bumps in sidewalks. This stroller came with a price tag of about $275. The second stroller we purchased was a lightweight, portable model that cost $50.

For the first few months, we used the larger carriage extensively. We lived in an area where we could take lovely, extended walks, and the baby could fully recline. Then, when our baby was five months old, we moved into a new home. Now to go for a long walk requires transporting both the baby and a stroller to a park or some other appropriate location. Suddenly, the "good" carriage stayed neatly covered in the garage and the "cheap" one went everywhere with us.

The moral of this story is to try and identify how you'll use an item before you purchase it.

I learned about strollers through a trial-and-error process, just like the car seats. I hope the information I've shared with you will help you avoid some of my blunders.

Diaper Bag

It's helpful to have some kind of diaper bag with compartments for transporting the enormous amount of baby gear you'll have when you go on outings with your newborn. There are many styles available, from the traditional baby prints to Chanel look-alikes. You'll have to decide what works best for you depending on where you'll be going and what you want slung over your shoulder when you get there. Some come with both carry handles and over-the-shoulder straps—the shoulder straps are a must!

Diapers (Cloth and disposable)

For some time now, there has been a big controversy about which is the more environmentally responsible choice of diaper. Much of it may depend upon where you live. Do you live in a part of the country where water shortages often occur? Then perhaps disposable diapers are a more politically correct choice for you. On the other hand, disposable diapers get added to our nation's landfills and take hundreds of years to break down, biodegradable or not. You'll have to listen to your own conscience on this one. There are persuasive arguments for both methods.

If you're concerned about cost, cloth diapers that you launder yourself may be the less expensive option. If you're not concerned about cost, there are cloth diaper services available almost everywhere. If you do choose disposable diapers, I recommend that you purchase a package of good-quality cloth diapers anyway to use as burping towels.

Knowing that you'll need to change your baby's diapers eight to twelve times a day (and if you didn't know that, you do now!), you may be tempted to go out and buy enough disposables to fill up your garage, basement, or whatever. My advice is: Don't do it! Babies come in many different sizes and shapes, and it's hard to tell how fast your infant will move into the next diaper size. Also, you may find that different brands fit your baby better at different times in their development.

In addition to fit, some babies are sensitive to the materials and chemicals used in making disposable diapers. Keep an eye out for rashes that may break out, and if they do, try another brand. National brands include Huggies, Luvs, Pampers, and Tushies. If generic brands work for your baby, they're often available at the best price.

Waterproof Pants for cloth diapers

If you decide to go the cloth diaper route, you'll need half a dozen waterproof pants. Both snap-on and pull-on styles are available. In my opinion, the snap-on style is easier to get on over a diaper. You might also investigate using Velcro-style diaper wraps, in which case you won't need to buy the next item on our list-diaper pins.

Safety Diaper Pins for Cloth Diapers

If you choose cloth diapers, look for the diaper pins that have locking heads. They prevent the pin from accidentally opening and sticking into your infant's tender skin.

Disposable Baby Wipes

Most of the disposable diaper manufacturers make baby wipes. National brands tend to be slightly more expensive than generic store brands. I suggest you consider a fragrance-free or hypoallergenic kind, particularly if your baby has very sensitive skin. Use the premoistened wipes sparingly (they're best for travel), because they may contribute to diaper rash. When changing a soiled diaper, use wipes first, then finish with a damp washcloth to remove any residue.

Baby Bottles

Like diapers, I strongly urge you not to overbuy, at least until you discover which type of bottle and nipple your baby likes. You basically have two choices: the standard bell-shaped nipple and the "orthodontic" Playtex nurser style, which some women say resembles a mother's nipple.

Bottles themselves are either plastic or glass and generally come in four- and eight-ounce sizes. You'll need a few bottles, even if you're breast-feeding, for those times when you want your partner to help with feeding or when you're away from home. At times when you're not nursing, your baby will need to feel comfortable using a bottle. National brands include Playtex, Evenflo, Gerber, and Johnson.

Bottle Brushes

Bottle brushes are generally a disposable item. To maintain a good level of sanitation, replace them every few months. Look for simple, sturdy ones at a good price.

Burping Towels

Many stores carry cute shoulder covers to use for burping your baby. Most do a good job of protecting your clothing and mopping up baby. However, they're usually more expensive than cloth diapers, which, as noted above, work extremely well for this purpose. In addition, many babies find them comforting to snuggle with. Should your baby develop an attachment to this kind of "blankie," they're easy to wash and replace without upsetting your baby with their absence.

Pacifiers

Pacifiers (aka Binkies and Nuks) sometimes help to satisfy a baby's natural sucking impulses, particularly between feedings and at sleep time. There is some controversy among pediatricians about the use of pacifiers, but most agree that a pacifier should not be used during the first two to three weeks of nursing. Once your baby's nursing skills are well established, giving your little one a pacifier becomes your choice.

Like bottle nipples, your baby may have a preference for a particular type of pacifier. Don't overbuy before you know what your baby's preference is. There are times and places when pacifiers can be lifesavers. If your baby becomes fussy, a pacifier can be an easy way to calm her when you're in public places and traveling by car or plane. Always throw away pacifiers when the nipples wear out or become sticky.

Receiving Blankets

These are lightweight blankets, typically of a cotton or cotton blend, and they come in many patterns, colors, and prices. You'll use them a lot in the beginning for swaddling, as a coverlet, a wrap, or a place to lie your baby. They're a versatile and essential piece of your new baby gear.

Waterproof Lap Pads

These can be of great assistance for protecting sheets, clothes, furniture, and upholstery, or anything else you want to keep dry. They're especially useful in the changing area when baby wets as you're removing a soiled diaper. (Trust me, it happens!) They also come in crib size and are invaluable for cutting down on laundry.

Cotton Swabs

Cotton swabs are for limited use. Initially, they're used only to clean the umbilical area. Use gently and with discretion. Never try to clean a baby's ear with a cotton swab. Your doctor will give you further guidance for their use.

Cotton Balls or Pads

These are handy for general, utilitarian functions such as cleaning and applying liquid products.

Rubbing Alcohol

This is used for cleaning the umbilical cord during the first two weeks of your baby's life. Use only as directed by your physician.

Barrier Cream

There are many brands available including Desitin, A&D and Balmex, to name a few. I recommend that you buy a small tube of more than one brand and see which you like best. At first, you may not need any cream, but it's good to have on hand, particularly if diaper rash occurs. Petroleum jelly (or Vaseline) was formerly used as a barrier cream, but there are many more suitable products available, and petroleum jelly is now primarily used for taking the baby's temperature rectally. You may want to have a small container on hand for this purpose.

Mild Shampoo or Cleansing Lotion

Newborn babies don't need daily bathing. Sponge bathing your newborn while he or she is wrapped in a warm towel is ordinarily sufficient during the first few weeks. Even when you do begin the bath, soap isn't necessary and may be detrimental to a newborn's sensitive skin. Therefore, purchase these products prudently. Consider those that are unscented, or use only a natural, mild fragrance.

Some baby brands are now offering fragrance-free and hypoallergenic products. I recommend these especially for young infants. Professional hair care products can be used as body wash. They meet skin pH requirements and have fewer of the ingredients that can be problematic. Professional product options include Redken, KMS, and Lanzé. Garden Botanica has a nice Herbal Baby Wash. Lines do come and go, so be sure to check the ingredients before buying any body care products for your baby.

Be an informed consumer! Read the labels carefully for ingredients in any products you buy for your baby. Many products labeled "for babies" have contents that you wouldn't consider using on yourself, so be sure you don't use them on your baby. Lanolin, for example, can be an irritant, and alcohol, which is often used in baby products, can be drying to many skin types.

Baby Bodysuit ("Onesies")

These are one-piece bodysuits with snaps at the crotch or waist. They can be worn alone in hot weather or under overalls, jumpers, or zippered sleepers in cold weather. Bodysuits stay in place better than regular shirts or T-shirts, but they may not be the most practical choice during the first few weeks of your newborn's life, considering they can be difficult to get over their heads. By the end of the first or second month, they'll be a great option.

T-Shirts

Babies detest having things that are pulled on and off over their heads. So when purchasing T-shirts, consider buying ones that tie or snap in the front or on the side, at least until your baby's neck becomes stronger. If you do select ones that go over the head, choose a style that has side snaps at the shoulder or a wide neck opening.

Footed Sleepers

Footed sleepers are convenient, anytime wear for newborns and infants. They're especially good for keeping your baby's feet warm and comfy. I recommend the ones with front and leg snaps for easier changing, and the more snaps, the better.

Drawstring Gowns

Drawstring gowns are best used as sleepwear. They're very convenient for Mom and comfortable for your baby during the first few months. They're also great for nighttime changing. As your infant becomes increasingly mobile, however, onepiece footed sleepers are more practical.

Baby Caps or Bonnets

Soft baby caps keep newborns cozy and warm while sleeping. Caps and bonnets are a good idea for infants when they're outdoors. They protect your baby from sun, wind, and cold.

Socks and Booties

Booties are good for keeping a baby's feet warm when they're wearing outfits that don't have feet in them already. Soft cotton socks function the same as booties, are good for everyday wear, and are less expensive. Consider your baby's comfort over fashion and select footwear that is appropriate for the weather and your baby's age.

Bibs

Last, but not least, we come to the washable bib! Most babies spit up and drool, some much more than others. If you want to protect your baby's clothing from becoming soiled and wet, bibs are the ticket, and they're much easier to change than a whole outfit. Bibs with snaps or Velcro fasteners can be taken on or off with less effort than those with ties. Rubber or plastic-backed types are great when infants start to eat solid foods or when she begins feeding herself.

Breast Pump

Breast pumps are available in a variety of forms, the simplest being a hand-operated single pump. The more deluxe model is an electric double pump. The latter is by far more efficient and time-saving. It's also the most expensive. Fortunately, they can be rented, typically through a hospital, breast feeding consultant, or some baby stores.. Unless the prices come down significantly, I recommend renting.

Breast pumps are convenient for all nursing mothers and essential for nursing working moms. They're indispensable if you need or want to share feeding responsibilities with your partner or child care person. In addition to providing some much needed freedom for a new mother, pumps can help to regulate your milk production.

Rocking Chair with Footstool

A rocking chair is a wonderful item to have from the time your child is a newborn until he or she is too big to hold. In the beginning, it's great for feeding and rocking your newborn to sleep. Then it becomes the perfect place to read stories to your child. A footstool is an added bonus for those precious moments when you can literally put your feet up and relax a bit yourself.

Camera/Video Equipment

A reliable auto-everything is the best bet for recording your first memories of your newborn. With all the activities that come with a new baby, the last thing you need to worry about is an f-stop setting. Keep some extra batteries and film on hand at all times. You won't want to miss that first smile!

Radio/Cassette/CD Player

Background music provides companionship sounds for your infant and minimizes other household noises. So it's a good idea to have it on when the baby naps during the day. Playing music in the baby's room also lets you know that the monitor is working.

Infant Swing

A swing provides a rhythmic motion to entertain and soothe your baby. Most babies love them. It's also another place for you to put your infant when you need free hands for other tasks. They either come in a mechanical windup or battery-powered model. Battery-operated models are quieter and run longer than windup styles.

Although battery-operated models may cost a bit more, they're beneficial especially for a sensitive baby who is disturbed by the noise of winding or a break in the motion. Some brands include a cradle and a seat. The cradle is generally used during only the first three to six weeks, so consider the length of time it'll be used when comparing prices.

Swings can be tipped over if they're bumped, so locate it in a safe place. Be sure to use the restraining belt provided with it and always keep an eye on your infant when he or she is swinging. There is some controversy about whether or not to leave your baby asleep in the swing. You'll have to evaluate the safety and tradeoffs for yourself. As soon as your baby reaches the weight limit for the swing, discontinue using it. Store it for your next one or lend it to a friend who is about to become a new parent.

Playpen or Port-a-Crib

A playpen is yet another safe place where your baby can play when she isn't sleeping, eating or being held. In fact, it's a good place for her to learn to entertain herself and experience some independence. For the amount of time you may use a playpen in your home and for travel, the smaller portable size (called a port-a-crib) should be adequate for most needs. Larger playpens are for more than one child to use simultaneously. You may not need to purchase a playpen and a portable crib, since they can serve the same purposes. The price for either is about the same.

Floor Quilt

A quilted blanket—some come with perimeter bumper pads-will contain a newborn/infant to a specific area on a bed or the floor. This item gives your baby a safe, clean place to stretch and move around on. It also protects your carpets and upholstery fabrics.

Infant Seat/Bouncie Seat

An infant seat is a comfortable place for baby to be and see all that you're doing. Some models have a molded seat and others are made of fabric with a flexible metal or plastic frame that reacts to the infant's movements with a gentle bouncing motion. There are battery-operated models that vibrate to soothe or help your baby to sleep. Never place the seat on an unstable surface or a high place where it can walk itself off the flat surface.

This is another place for an infant where she can stretch and wiggle safely while you do other things. This gives the baby an opportunity to sit up and see what's going on around them, including keeping an eye on you!

Crib Mobile

A crib mobile provides amusement and visual stimulation for your newborn. It also adds decoration to your baby's room. Those with high-contrast colors provide more visual stimulation than pastels. Some mobiles contain battery-operated or wind-up music boxes.

A mobile becomes a favorite target for babies to pull on as soon as they're old enough to reach or pull themselves up to a standing position, so hang it out of your child's reach and remove it when your baby is able to grab it. Crib mobiles are primarily aesthetic.

If you're trying to stay within your budget and must choose between a crib play board or a mirror toy and a mobile, I believe your baby will get more enjoyment and longer use from a play board or mirror toy than the mobile. If possible, borrow these items to see which your baby prefers before you purchase any.

Crib Mirror

Crib mirrors can be purchased alone or as part of an activities board. For safety purposes, select a mirror that's specifically designed for babies. Typically, mirrors are one of the first play items to attract a baby's attention.

Crib Animal with Intrauterine Sounds

This is a stuffed animal, such as a rock-a-bye bear or bunny, with an internal music box that plays sounds that are similar to those heard in the womb, or so the manufacturers of these toys claim. They're designed to be soothing for sensitive or fussy infants during the first few weeks. How long your baby will use this item is questionable, but if it helps keep your baby happy in those first few weeks, it's well worth it.

Music Box

Music boxes come in a variety of shapes and sizes. Most play one melody—familiar tunes such as *Twinkle, Twinkle, Little Star* or *Rock a Bye Baby*. Many babies find music boxes both soothing and entertaining.

Baby Toys

Visual stimulation is the first type of interaction a baby has with toys. There are many black-and-white and high-contrast colored items available as mobiles, flash cards that hang or sit near the baby, rattles, stuffed animals, and more. Unlike the toys of previous generations that were soft colored and shaped, research has proven that these nontraditional educational toys are effective stimulation and babies love them.

When choosing stuffed animals, consider buying ones that are small, soft, squishy—and washable! They're the best for newborns, who are just beginning to grasp things. Use caution when selecting stuffed animals, though. Many have eyes, noses, buttons, or other parts that can come off and seriously injure a baby if swallowed. If you receive stuffed animals as gifts, check them over thoroughly before giving them to your child and take off any loose or removable details.

Some babies prefer smooth plastic or wooden items, so I recommend that you experiment with a few playthings before buying several of any kind. If you're having any showers, toys are a favorite shower and baby gift. This is another reason not to spend a lot of money on toys too early in the game.

I've always found it remarkable that no matter how many toys you buy for them, many babies are happy entertaining themselves with a couple of wooden spoons or plastic measuring cups that fit inside one another. Trust me, as your child gets older, they'll give you endless opportunities to buy them many toys if you so desire!

Clothes Hamper

A clothes hamper is handy for your baby's soiled clothes. Even if you have one for yourself, another basket for your infant's clothes will save you a lot of frustration when you're trying to separate wash loads or locate a particular item.

Baby Wipe Warner

If you use baby wipes, a warmer will keep them at a cozy temperature near to your baby's body temperature. Often when people first hear of these warmers, they consider them a silly extravagance. However, they're especially helpful when you're trying to keep an infant sleepy and calm during a late-night diaper change. At 10 A.M. it may simply be a convenience, but it's a lifesaver at 2 A.M. when you really need to get some sleep!

Washcloths

Most baby washcloths are of a lighter weight fabric and smaller in size than adult ones. They're used during bathing and for cleaning your baby's bottom during diaper changing. Having two colors or patterns will make it easy to identify which washcloths are for the baby's top and which are for baby's bottom.

Hooded Baby Towels

Like washcloths, hooded baby towels are smaller and lighter weight than their adult counterparts. This makes them more manageable with a small infant. Although these items are handy, they're not essential if you're trying to stick to a budget.

Towel sets are a great shower gift, so put them on your wish list and wait until after your shower to purchase them yourself. When buying baby towels, choose those with a tighter weave and avoid the thinner, flimsy ones. The ones that are very thin roll up and become oddly shaped after only a few washings.

Baby Carrier or Backpack

There are several styles of baby packs, backpacks, and slings. Baby packs are soft, pouchlike carriers that convert from carrying the baby facing inward to facing outward. A newborn should be carried in front until his or her neck has the strength to stay up on its own. Older babies can use a framed backpack once they're able to sit up or push up to standing on their own.

Babies love being carried in baby packs because they feel secure and warm, and they can hear the heartbeat and breathing of the person carrying them. If you have a baby with colic or other similar conditions, a baby pack may be the only way you'll ever get anything done other than hold your baby. Baby catalogs and stores have a variety of styles to choose from. They come in many colors and fabrics. Check the stitching, cleaning method, and sturdiness of any baby carrier before purchasing it.

Car Window Shade

Another wonderful modern convenience is the car window shade. These are portable items that protect your baby from direct sunlight and the discomfort it can bring to your baby. It's a good idea to keep one in each car.

Strap Covers and Head Supports for Car Seat

Terry cloth covers with Velcro fasteners for your car seat's safety straps provide additional comfort for your infant, especially when sleeping, and are much easier to clean than the safety straps themselves. It's amazing how soiled these straps become in a short time. Recently, I've seen strap wing supports that keep a baby's head supported while sleeping. The strap covers may do for the first few weeks, but the supports will be used from then on for another two to three years. You'll thank yourself many times over for this purchase. I certainly did the second time around—I didn't have them for my first child.

Doughnut Head Cushion for Car Seat

This type of cushion is used to support your baby's head much like an adult travel pillow, except that it sits under their chin. I recommend the softest one available. If the pillow is too firm, it may be difficult to get it on and off your infant's neck and will be less helpful. Like the wing supports, its purpose is to provide stability for your baby's head when traveling in a vehicle. It also prevents their head and neck from being in an awkward position for long periods of time. A rolled towel or blanket can serve the same purpose, but the doughnut pillow or wing supports are much more convenient.

Day Wear Outfits

For newborns I strongly recommend simple one-piece outfits for daily wear and sleepwear. Simple terry cloth or cotton onesies and bodysuits with feet that have front snaps from top to bottom are great! Your baby may go through several of these outfits in a day, so stay with easy, inexpensive, washable items for everyday at-home wear. For special occasions, you may choose to splurge on something more fancy. Just remember to include a bib with the ensemble.

Crib Shoes

Crib shoes are mainly decorative and may be used for special occasions. For daily wear, soft cotton or terry cloth socks are much more practical and comfortable for your baby.

Bunting (Zip or Button)

Buntings are quilt-like blankets that zip or button to create a baby envelope or sleeping bag. They're wonderful in cold weather. You can dress your infant in bodysuits and socks and slip her into a bunting to keep her cozy and warm. Most buntings can be unzipped or unbuttoned and converted into a quilt to lay your baby on or cover her with. Before purchasing a bunting, check for the essential car seat buckle slit. (It's much like a large buttonhole.) Buntings are a lovely convenience in temperate climates but are more essential in chilly weather.

SURVEYING THE OUTFITTERS

Now that you know what you need, where do you get it?! What follows are the primary destinations for acquiring the baby gear I outlined for you. There are advantages and disadvantages to each type of store, so find out what's available in your community and target the ones that suit your requirements.

WHERE TO LOOK

Baby Boutiques. Baby boutiques are wonderful places for getting an overview of what's available and new on the market. These stores tend to be smaller—they carry national brands, locally made or specialty items, one-of-a-kind items, and limited editions. Boutiques are more likely to carry handmade and imported goods. Overall, most small boutiques focus on clothing and great gift items—not furniture. Items you purchase here tend to be pricier. If you shop the sales, you may get a good value on quality clothing or specialty items, but don't expect to find many bargains!

Full-Service Baby Stores. From Bellini to John Doe's Baby Barn, stores like this carry a full range of furniture, clothing, and supplies. The high-end stores carry exclusive, imported, or domestic merchandise, while others offer value-priced and budget-minded goods—or a combination of both. Compare the prices on standard items to get a truer picture of what range of pricing a particular store falls into.

A full-service store will generally have a larger supply of items in stock but have the ability to special order items if they're not in stock. Full-service baby stores are great for people who value one-stop shopping. Buyers may pay slightly higher prices than they would at a club or discount store, but for some people the convenience is well worth it.

Department Stores. The scope of department stores is vast—we're talking Wal-Mart to Nordstrom! The store's image is reflected in its prices and the quality of its merchandise. Some department stores, like Nordstrom, carry only clothing and gift items, while others carry a full range of furniture and supplies as well. Sears is a good example of this.

On-line Shopping. One of the newest ways to shop for you and your baby is on the Internet. If you happen to be on bed rest, this can be a wonderful opportunity for mom to participate in the shopping without leaving her bedroom. Whether you actually make your purchases or not, it's a great way to browse and do your window-shopping. Gap, Macy's, Toy "R" Us, Target and Wal-Mart are just a few of the on-line sites available.

Club Stores. Club stores refer to places like Price Club/Costco, Sam's, and others. Merchandise in these stores varies from month to month, if not week to week. Club stores have competitive prices on equipment like car seats, port-a-cribs, and strollers. If they have an item in stock when you're in the market for it, chances are you won't find it cheaper anywhere else. Since the merchandise changes constantly, you'll need to check the stock frequently if you're looking for something specific. If you see what you want, buy it now! It probably won't be there in a week or two.

Club stores also have good prices on economy-sized items or cases of things like diapers, formula, baby wipes, and jars of baby food. Do compare the unit price with your local supermarket to see if the price difference is enough to justify purchasing the larger quantity. Remember, you've got to have enough storage space to hold it all!

Nearly New Stores. Used items are found in secondhand or nearly new stores. Some of these stores do carry new items as well. Generally, the prices are unbeatable if they happen to have what you need and like. Some nearly new stores carry only clothing, while others have a variety of furniture and other gear such as car seats, high chairs, and strollers. The best items go fast, so if you want the real bargains, you'll need to shop these stores on a regular basis. To find terrific deals on great gear, having the time and the inclination to shop is a must.

Rummage/Yard Sales. If you're already an experienced rummage "sailor," then you know how to find the bargains shopping this way. As with the nearly new stores, if you enjoy the process and have the time, you can buy virtually all the basics for next to nothing.

> *If you haven't shopped this way in the past but would like to try, check your local newspaper for rummage or yard sales in the classified ads section. Sales usually take place on weekends, so it's best to look in the Friday and Saturday papers. Search for ads listing baby items or the specific things you're looking for. Get to the sale early—again, the best items go fast.*

Successful rummage-sale buying is a combination of timing, persistence, and a bit of luck. I was able to purchase a Child Craft convertible bed in great condition for $250 through a classified ad. The woman still had the sales receipt. They paid $650 for it!

Loan Items and Hand-Me-Downs. If you don't have the urge to splurge or the financial resources to buy everything, then loaners from friends and relatives are like manna from heaven. If I had to make a choice, I'd take items for a newborn through the first year. Babies grow so fast during this time that the clothes don't fit for very long and the developmental changes are amazing. So for toys and everyday wear items, borrow everything you can! Most mothers are happy to have someone to lend or pass on their baby things to—and this applies to more than just clothes. Cradles, bassinets, swings, and so on can be valuable contributions, not to mention a lifesaver to your budget.

Some items and equipment will be as good as new by simply replacing the cushion or adding a fresh cover. It's much less expensive than buying a new item altogether. Another benefit of borrowing is that you have a chance to see what things your baby likes before you purchase an item.

If the lender wants her things returned, take only the items you really like and think you can return in good condition. If you become a lender at some point, entrust only those items you don't intend to have as keepsakes. Both you and the user would feel terrible if a favorite treasure was spoiled or lost.

> *Rummage sale items and hand-me-downs of any kind can be safety risks, especially when it comes to things like cradles, cribs, playpens, and the like. Look these items over carefully before you borrow or buy them. Current product and government safety regulations did not apply to many items produced some years ago, as they do now.*

Miscellaneous. Toys "R" Us carries a trainload of gear besides toys. It has an extensive inventory of baby gear and supplies ranging from cribs and car seats to diapers and formula. Make sure you cross the threshold of Toys "R" Us armed with a prioritized shopping list, price comparisons, and lots of time to browse. A large variety of products and competitive prices will make a trip there well worth your while.

Note, however, that clothing items should not be your primary objective here. Items like bibs and T-shirts are generally in good supply and are value priced, but most apparel isn't of the highest quality.

Drug stores like Long's and Save-On usually carry a good inventory of everyday needs such as diapers, formula, bibs, socks, bottles, and other accessories. Take advantage of the sales in these stores whenever possible. They can be great money-savers if you catch a good sale.

Last word! The best values on clothing and other gear are found by purchasing quality items on sale at high-quality, upper-end stores.

Baby Showers. Baby showers are a wonderful tradition! They're like bachelorette parties, except they're for pregnant women having a last fling before settling into the responsibilities of parenthood. Some are lavish, with extraordinary decorations, centerpieces, generous spreads of food, and lots of activities.

Others are understated gatherings of friends, relatives, and coworkers. I highly recommend you enjoy as many showers as are offered to you. After six or seven months of pregnancy, you've earned at least one great party!

If you and your partner have several friends who enjoy being together, a couples shower can be lots of fun. This is done somewhat differently than the traditional all-girls baby shower—it's more like a birthday party or barbecue. It's one more way to include your partner in an experience that may enhance your parenting partnership.

If you have several friends and relatives who want to host showers for you, separate your guest list appropriately. With close friends and coworkers, keep the size of the group limited to six to twelve people per party. This will give you a better opportunity to interact with all of your guests. If the attendees are casual acquaintances and friends of your mother-in-law, for example, a larger gathering may work well.

Baby shower activities and games range from fun and informative to silly and embarrassing. If you want to use the time to socialize or solicit information from other experienced mothers, let your hostess know in advance so she can plan accordingly. Anyone who is kind and generous enough to throw a shower for you will appreciate knowing your preferences about the menu and activities.

In regard to shower gifts, many hostesses will ask you for your wish list. Don't be shy about doing this! Think about what you want and need and then return the list promptly. If you choose not to honor this request, don't be surprised when you get six stuffed animals, duplicates of things you don't need and will have to exchange, and nothing else. Consider asking for a group gift—a larger item such as a stroller, car seat, or bumper set. This allows the guests to share the cost of a more expensive item that they know you need and appreciate. More often than not, people prefer to give gifts that are genuinely valued and just happen to look wonderful when they're unwrapped at a party.

Many baby stores have shower registries similar to bridal registries. This is an option that is becoming more and more popular with expectant mothers, especially when the shower host doesn't request a wish list from the mother-to-be.

One of the best ideas I've heard lately concerning baby showers is from a woman who circulated a sign-up sheet at the shower whereby those who signed up volunteered to provide a meal for the new family during the first six weeks after the baby arrived home.

Participants agreed to deliver a meal in a disposable container that came ready to eat or freeze. Each vowed not to cross the threshold of the new mother's home unless they were prepared to provide some type of essential domestic service immediately upon entering!

SUMMARY

 Experience is an amazing thing. It brings with it a tremendous amount of practical wisdom. So here are some words of wisdom about buying baby stuff. With few exceptions like car seats and cribs, rocking chairs and furniture, most of the clothing and entertainment items you'll purchase are only going to be used for a few weeks or a few months. So when you're deciding what to buy, consider the item's price relative to how long or how often you or your baby will use the item. There are special things like christening gowns or family heirlooms I exclude from this comment.

 As time goes by, you'll become more familiar with the baby stores in your area as well as your child's individual needs. Shopping with your baby will replace the recreational shopping you enjoyed during pregnancy and pre-pregnancy days. You'll be amazed at how efficient you become at locating the items you want. Getting in and getting out quickly will become the supreme objective.

 In retrospect, my biggest mistake was overbuying clothing at the sales. I was often disappointed when purchases I had made with the future in mind didn't fit at the right time the next year. Frequently, I overbought the bargains for a particular season, and many of the items were hardly used. It's difficult to successfully buy ahead, since there's no way of knowing exactly what size or "transportation mode" your little one will be in when the right season comes around again. Most children's stores are great about returns when you have a receipt, so keep them somewhere easy to find.

 Brands such as Baby Gap, Gymboree and OshKosh are excellent clothing values, particularly when they're on sale. But times do change and quality can vary, so ask other mothers with children of similar age or slightly older children what brands are working well for them.

 In my experience, there is rarely a shortage of darling clothes and paraphernalia for kids. I recommend you buy fewer things for each season and phase that your child is in and only purchase the things you really love. This way you can have fun buying something new as the seasons change and your baby grows. I reached the conclusion that quantity is not necessarily more satisfying—and with clothing, it simply means more laundry to do.

Shower Wish List
for

_____

Colors: _____

Nursery Theme: _____

Group Items: _____

Needs	*Wants*
_____	_____
_____	_____
_____	_____
_____	_____
_____	_____
_____	_____
_____	_____
_____	_____
_____	_____
_____	_____
_____	_____
_____	_____
_____	_____
_____	_____
_____	_____
_____	_____
_____	_____
_____	_____
_____	_____

Shower Gift Thank You List

Shower: **Date:**

Hostess:

Gift Item	*Name*	*Address*

Shower Gift: Meal Delivery Sign-Up Sheet

Favorites:

Things to avoid:

Directions: Please deliver meals ready to warm and eat or put in the freezer. Use disposable containers or attach a note stating that you do not want the container returned. Call ahead to determine a delivery time and leave food at the door unless otherwise requested. Thanks for participating.

Sign Up for a Day

SUN	MON	TUES	WED	THURS	FRI	SAT

Preparing for Life
After Birth

Chapter 4

Preparing for Life
After Birth

Some expectant parents have Hallmark and Hollywood fantasies of what pregnancy and becoming parents is all about. Most of those ideas should probably remain where they came from—on the big screen and in the greeting card shops. Babies do provide many precious moments but one's expectations need to be tempered with a little reality.

Many first-time parents spend an inordinate amount of time and energy preparing for delivery and forget about the first few weeks at home with their newborn. In fact, it's the first three to five weeks at home that often prove to be the most overwhelming and an extremely challenging experience. There is probably no way to be completely ready for the arrival of your first child. However, this section is full of practical and effective tips to help you navigate successfully through your pregnancy, delivery, and coming home with your first baby.

In this chapter I'll cover a lot of ground, beginning with managing your pregnancy and delivery and then moving on to an in-depth look at preparing for your post-delivery recovery. This includes ways for new mothers to stay aware of their needs as well as their newborn's.

There are many things that happen before, during, and after delivery that your doctor won't think to talk about because they're so routine for her or him. You might get some of this information from a close girlfriend who has had a baby recently, but most likely she's too busy to fill you in on the details—or she doesn't want to dampen your spirits by being too specific or graphic. But the fact is that you'll be glad to have all the information you can when it's your turn to deliver and bring home your baby.

Since many of these topics are not exactly what people are comfortable talking about in any case, I thought it vital that I cover the general items common to most women. Postpartum, for example, the time immediately following delivery through the next several weeks or months, involves the physical and emotional adjustment from pregnancy to parenthood. This important information will help you keep things in perspective and not only survive the most difficult moments but maybe even laugh a bit. Well, take a deep breath, now you head into basic survival training.

GUIDING YOUR PREGNANCY AND DELIVERY

Most women have a gynecologist, but if you've just found out you're pregnant, you may not have a gynecologist who delivers babies. You have many choices of health care practitioners to manage your pregnancy and delivery. The various options include obstetricians, family practitioners, certified or licensed nurse-midwives, and perinatologists.

Interview your candidates and ask pertinent questions. For example, if you want to do a home birth using a midwife, you'll need to find out if your obstetrician will work with you on this plan. Most hospitals now have birthing rooms that allow you to labor and deliver in one place. Does your hospital? Most importantly, if a problem arises, will your practitioner refer you to the appropriate specialist? Did you know that some obstetricians don't perform their own C-sections? Will your practitioner work with a perinatologist? For more information, you can contact the associations listed in the appendix. They'll help you locate qualified individuals who will assist you in accomplishing your birthing goals while maintaining a safe environment for you and your baby.

Having given birth twice, I'm convinced that every pregnant woman must be her own advocate and an active participant on her health care team if she means to complete the baby adventure happy, healthy, and fulfilled. With your first pregnancy, there may be a tendency to let the medical practitioner you've chosen lead the way and make decisions for you because you think he or she knows best. Keep in mind that your health care provider is a human being, not all-knowing or all-powerful. On occasion, just like the rest of us, doctors forget things we've told them and can even make mistakes.

You'll be well served to ask questions, read all the pertinent information, and monitor your body's changes and reactions throughout your pregnancy. If you're uncomfortable with a recommended procedure or prescription, discuss options and inquire about the benefits and risks before going ahead.

HAVING YOUR FIRST BABY WHEN YOU'RE OVER THIRTY-FIVE

More and more women are waiting until later in life to have babies. With medical technology what it is today, it's becoming more common for women well into their thirties and forties to bring a baby safely into the world. However, be advised that pregnancies later in life often require medical tests and procedures not generally needed for women under thirty years of age.

If you're embarking on this journey and you're over thirty-five, it's standard practice to have an amniocentesis. This procedure extracts a small amount of amniotic fluid to check for possible genetic and fetal disorders. Its primary function is to find out if your baby has Down's syndrome. Before you undergo this procedure, consider the following:

- Amniocentesis, like most other prenatal diagnostic testing, should be done only when the benefits outweigh the risks.

- Although rare, the testing procedure can cause leakage of amniotic fluid, and there is a slight risk of accidentally pricking the fetus with the needle. (Currently, amnios are done with the aid of ultrasound to avoid touching the baby.)

- If the test is positive and your baby has Down's syndrome or some other abnormality, what course of action will you take?

- If the test is positive, will knowing help you prepare for your baby's special needs or will it put you under too much stress for the remainder of your pregnancy?

ESTIMATED TIME OF ARRIVAL

Babies are inclined to come when they're good and ready; therefore, due dates are not necessarily certain. Due dates are based upon when your last menstrual cycle began or when you last ovulated, if you're monitoring that. The more precise your date of conception, the more accurate your projected delivery date will be.

When it comes to delivery time, there are good reasons for letting nature take its course, especially with regard to having babies. But there are times when intervention such as inducing labor or performing a Cesarean section is the best option. You should speak with your practitioner about the risks and benefits of labor induction and Cesarean sections before you're faced with a decision about either one.

One reason for inducing labor, or delivering a baby early, has to do with the size and weight of the baby in relation to the size and bone structure of the mother. In some cases, a full-term baby will be too large for the mother to deliver vaginally. This can be monitored by ultrasound and physical examination. Infections and other medical conditions that cause fetal stress or complications for the mother could precipitate intervention and an early delivery. Fortunately, these are rare situations. With good medical care, chances are greatly in your favor that you'll have a normal, vaginal delivery. However, should one of these uncommon circumstances occur, in most cases it will be managed favorably with today's phenomenal medical technology.

EXPERIENCE TALKS

For about nine months, your body goes through changes while it's nurturing your baby and preparing for childbirth. Soon you'll be on your way to the hospital counting the minutes, then seconds, between contractions. What you may have forgotten to pack won't be the first thing on your mind, especially if the beginning of labor has taken you by surprise—which it often does for many couples, no matter how prepared they think they are.

Others of you may already have packed a steamer trunk full of goodies that has been positioned by the door for the last several weeks. Although this may have seemed like a good idea at the time, someone is going to have to move all that stuff at least once during your hospital stay. Fortunately, it won't be you. Don't overpack. Hopefully, this isn't going to be an extended visit. Although it may not have been the case when your mother delivered you, hospitals now provide almost everything you'll need. With the exception of your own toothbrush and similar personal items, you might as well use what the hospital provides; you're paying for it!

I've compiled lists for both mom and dad of the items I suggest you take to the hospital to get you through this next part of the adventure as comfortably as possible. (See pages 83 and 84.)

CESAREAN SECTION

The reasons for a Cesarean birth, or C-section, are many: the mother's health, fetal stress, when the baby's head is too large for the mother's pelvic structure, the baby's position in the uterus is not favorable, or when labor is prolonged by ineffective contractions. There are many reasons why a fast, surgical delivery would be reasonable.

Over the years, C-sections have been viewed in various ways, ranging from a life-saving procedure to an alternative for those not wishing to experience labor and a vaginal delivery. A C-section may sound like an easy way to avoid labor and vaginal delivery, when in fact it's major abdominal surgery and should be taken seriously. It involves all the usual recovery issues such as longer hospitalization, abdominal pain, and loss of muscle strength.

In my opinion, what is to be avoided at all costs is going twenty-four hours or more in hard labor and then having a C-section. Vaginal labor and delivery or a C-section is challenging enough all by itself. Why struggle another twelve or twenty-four hours and then have a C-section? Having to do both is extremely taxing physically and mentally, so save your strength for your recovery and caring for your newborn baby. You'll need all the stamina and energy you can muster. If you reach twelve hours of hard labor and haven't delivered yet, talk to your health care professional about your options, including a C-section. Weigh the benefits and risks of a Cesarean with your practitioner. If he or she is convinced it's necessary, you or your baby's life may depend on it.

EPISIOTOMY

An episiotomy is an incision made from the vagina downward toward the anus during the final stages of childbirth. Ugh! I couldn't even hear the word "episiotomy" without cringing and becoming slightly nauseated (and that's before I was pregnant!). In actual fact, the thought of the procedure was far worse than the real-life experience. Thankfully, my episiotomy turned out to be minor for both deliveries. With the help of an epidural and the thinning of the tissues, all I felt was the faint sting when the local anesthetic was injected.

Doctors have strong opinions regarding the use of an episiotomy. There are pros and cons to both having and not having one. It's to your advantage to know your doctor's bias long before delivery. However, my experience suggests that a clean surgical incision, properly stitched, heals much faster than a serious tear of those delicate membranes. You'll have to make this assessment for yourself.

PREPARING FOR DELIVERY

Quite honestly, I was terrified about the prospect of delivering my first baby. The thought of childbirth had frightened me ever since I learned how babies entered this world. Nevertheless, by the time delivery of my first newborn came around, I was so ready to be un-pregnant that I decided I could get through just about anything for one day. I told myself, *One day vs. nine months of vomiting—how bad can it be?* I wish I could tell you it was a glorious experience. For me it wasn't, but with the help of some sympathetic and well-trained nurses, anesthesiologists, and my doctor, it went much smoother than I expected, and the sight of my baby daughter was truly a spectacular moment!

Today, women have many good options, far more than in previous generations, when it comes to labor, delivery, and after baby's arrival, so take time to investigate them. For example, do you want a home birth, or would you prefer delivering your baby in a birthing center at the hospital? Do you or your partner want to cut the umbilical cord, or should the doctor? These kinds of questions will come up if you take a birthing class or read a book like *Your Pregnancy: Every Woman's Guide* by Glade B. Curtis, M.D., OB/GYN, or *What to Expect When You're Expecting* by Arlene Eisenberg, et al. It's worth your time and effort to be informed about the choices you have in delivery options, along with their benefits and risks.

Some women choose to write a birth plan to help them manage their delivery—wonderful! However, it's vital to keep an open mind and a flexible attitude because it's impossible to predict exactly how your labor and delivery will go. I highly recommend you take a birthing class at your hospital, through your health care provider's office, or through a qualified program like Lamaze. These classes cover in depth many birthing methods and issues and will help you base your decisions on good information and personal preferences.

The choices you make must be made with you and your baby's health and safety as the top priority. It's important that your significant other knows your preferences because he and the nursing staff will be with you throughout the majority of your labor and delivery. Routinely, your doctor arrives in the final stages of labor, just a short time before the actual delivery.

Hopefully, your partner will be the calm one during stressful times and be able to communicate your preferences and needs to the health care team.

Including your partner in the decision-making process during the early stages of your pregnancy is a wonderful way to acknowledge his role as a teammate from the start. This will add to his confidence and enhance his ability to be your advocate when you need him most. Making pregnancy and delivery decisions together from the start will enrich the overall birthing experience and further establish a partnership approach to parenting.

The most important issues to cover with your doctor include your concerns about complications such as an unexpected Cesarean section and your preferences for pain medication, , an episiotomy, and having time with your new baby before he or she is taken away to the nursery. Accompanying your baby to the nursery for weighing and initial check-in is a special experience.

My husband found this activity to be truly wonderful, and I believe it contributed significantly to his bonding process with both our children.

I have a girlfriend who delivers her babies naturally in just a few hours. About an hour and one-half after she delivers, she's ready to shower and go home! I guarantee you, this is not the norm. If it happens—celebrate! It'll be like winning the lottery!

The following lists are designed to help you sort out what you actually need to take with you to the hospital when delivery time finally arrives.

Mom's List of Things to Take to the Hospital

- Bathrobe and slippers (no fancy negligees, please!)

- Nightgowns, knee length or shorter, and washable; ones designed for nursing are most convenient (or a shorter top will do); or use the gowns the hospital provides

- Cotton or cotton-lined underpants (choose your most inexpensive ones)

- Nursing bras and pads (two bras is a good idea)

- Lotion for massaging your back and legs

- Glasses or contact lenses (with any solutions you use)

- Toiletries (shampoo, hair brush, hair dryer, soap, deodorant, toothpaste, toothbrush, cosmetics, moisturizers, hair fasteners, perfume, and anything else you consider essential)

- Moisturizing lip balm

- Warm socks for cold feet

- Address book, note pad, pen, or pencil

- Tape/CD player and music, if it helps you relax (optional)

- Loose-fitting outfit to wear home (early maternity size should do)

- Going-home clothes and blankets for the baby (weather-appropriate and comfy, please)

- Car seat for baby's ride home

Dad's List of Things to Take to the Hospital

- Insurance card

- Plenty of change to make phone calls and for snack machines (a phone or credit card will work, too, for the phone calls)

- List of calls to make to friends and relatives

- Your favorite sandwich or snacks (optional; I guess it depends on how well you like your hospital's food)

- Film, camera, video camera if desired (throw in some extra batteries)

- A special gift for Mom (jewelry is always a big hit, but flowers are nice, too!)

- A great deal of fortitude!

SURVIVAL TIPS FOR NEW MOMS

ARRANGING HELP FROM FAMILY AND FRIENDS

There are a few general tasks that can be accomplished before Mom and the baby arrive home from the hospital that will make life a little less hectic during the initial onset of parenthood. I've already discussed some of the items you'll need to stock up on for the baby. Unless you have a full-time housekeeper who shops for you (wouldn't that be nice!), a home office assistant to pay your bills (that'd be nice, too!), then Dad is probably the best candidate to take care of the following details:

DAD'S TO-DO LIST

- **Buy groceries.** Yes, you'll want to eat, too! Stock up on some easy things to prepare. (My husband highly recommends big boxes of cereal and large quantities of milk.) Better yet, prepare some meals ahead of time and freeze them. Put them in containers that you can pop into the oven or microwave.

- **Pay bills.** Pay your bills for the coming month so you won't have to do it once the baby is at home. Seemingly small chores such as this can become an unnecessary burden with the new demands you'll have when your baby comes home. As soon as you settle into your new life, routine tasks will become just that again—routine.

- **Double check to see that all the medical supplies for Mom are at hand.** (Tucks, sanitary napkins, Dermaplast, nursing pad, etc.)

- **If you're using a diaper service or baby nurse, inform both of the baby's arrival.** Instruct the diaper service when to begin delivering diapers.

- **Change sheets on Mom and Dad's bed.** This isn't something a new mom should be doing right away, and you'll both appreciate getting into your own comfy bed with fresh sheets after your hospital stay.

EXTENDED FAMILY MATTERS . . . AND FRIENDS

As you think about how you'd like to spend those first weeks at home with your new baby, please consider thoughtfully who you'd like to share this precious time with. You and your partner may want to spend the first days or weeks alone with your new infant. If it's not possible for your mate to stay home with you at least part of the time, have a close friend or relative come to help with the domestic chores and provide you with companionship while you're settling in.

Whatever approach you take, the needs of your new family must take precedence over what other extended family members and friends may request. Therefore, think prudently before making commitments to anyone regarding your baby's first week or two at home. Although situations differ from couple to couple, here are some thoughts to reflect upon as you prepare to handle the onslaught of benevolence that will undoubtedly be offered by family and friends.

- Foremost, there should be no such thing as a "guest" during the first few weeks at home with your newborn. You need to surround yourself with those who are quick to perform any and all domestic chores without provocation and are delighted to help in any way they can.

- Enthusiastic mothers and mothers-in-law often talk about when they should visit long before you begin to show a belly. Are these mothers easy keepers or are they high maintenance? Can they take care of themselves and help with routine household chores without you asking? Do your families visit you often? Are they familiar with your local area and your household activities? In short, can they get to the grocery store and back on their own? If so, they may be good candidates as helpers during the first few weeks after your baby's arrival. If not, suggest they come three or four weeks after you return home.

- Your health and stamina are vital resources that must be protected and replenished. Although you may experience an adrenaline high during the first few days, your body will probably need a lot of rest and recuperation. The type of delivery you have may greatly impact your physical condition. Even a normal delivery demands a tremendous amount of physical strength and endurance. A protracted labor, C-section, or other complication can dramatically reduce your energy and physical resources. If your partner is willing and able to take time off from his work and cover the domestic chores for a week to ten days, I highly recommend it. If not, you'll have to choose another candidate. Do not expect that you can do it all yourself.

- Unless you have a guest room, don't even offer to have family or friends stay with you during their visit. Everyone needs privacy at times, and new babies tend to cry—frequently in the wee hours of the morning. It's better to have a couple of well-rested people around than a room full of zombies.

- Don't expect to get along differently, or better, with your family or in-laws just because there's a new baby. Any aberrant good behavior lasts only a few hours or at most a couple of days. Then it's back to business as usual in terms of family dynamics. The flip side of this is that I've personally never heard of a new baby who destroyed a healthy family relationship.

- You may enjoy the hustle and bustle of family and friends around you while you're in the glow of your newborn. Some couples thrive on this kind of lifestyle at whatever moment it is. More power to you! Just be sure not to overdo it for you or your newborn. The consequences of exhaustion for you or your infant can be severe.

ESSENTIALS FOR AT-HOME RECOVERY

The greatest danger I see for new moms is trying to do too much, much too soon. What is most undermining is not the perpetual demands of your newborn, but your own attempt to keep doing everything you were doing before the baby came, and more.

May I clue you in on a couple of things, before you even contemplate the following? (I know, because you hear every new mom talk about these things.) Thank you notes for gifts will be appreciated regardless of whether you send them in a week or two months. Domestic chores—forget about them! You'll have the opportunity to clean the house and do the laundry until the next millennium—so why start any sooner than you have to? This applies to cooking, too. In fact, don't try to do anything domestic.

Your baby is a newborn for only the first four to six weeks of their life. Don't miss this precious time by trying to be Wonder Woman. Relax and let other people take care of you while you take care of your baby. With the possible exception of having another baby, this may be the last time you'll get this kind of treatment for years to come, so enjoy it!

TEN COMMANDMENTS FOR THE POSTPARTUM MOTHER

1. Thou shalt not cook, clean thy house, do laundry, or be expected to amuse others

2. Thou shalt be given a doula. ("Doula" is from the Greek word meaning "a maidservant." Today she's a supportive person who is professionally trained to provide labor support and postpartum care for the mother and the newborn.) In other words, you shall seek relief in the form of a helper, housekeeper, or someone who will take care of you. Friends and relatives shall be deemed well suited.

3. Thou shalt remain dressed in thy nightgown and seated in thy rocking chair for as long as thou chooseth.

4. Thou shalt honor thy husband with his share of household chores.

5. Thou shalt not have slothful visitors in thy home.

6. Thou shalt take long walks in green pastures, eat good grub, and drink copious amounts of water.

7. Thou shalt groom thy hair and adorn thy body with attractive robes and other garments (the ones that fit comfortably).

8. Thou shalt not give thy baby to ill-suited persons or incompetent ones.

9. Thou shalt not listen to prophets of bad baby advice, including kinsfolk and other acquaintances.

10. Thou shalt sleep when thy baby sleeps!

All kidding aside, the postpartum period is a time of immense change and adjustment. Your hormones are working overtime. And your body is recuperating from enormous changes. It's essential that you acknowledge your emotional side during this time as well as your physical side. Talk about the feelings you're experiencing with those you trust and respect. It may amaze you how quickly and frequently your emotions will soar and plummet. So go easy on yourself.

One of the most soothing postpartum experiences I encountered during my hospital recovery period was a sitz bath. If you're not familiar with it, it's like a small whirlpool for your tushie. It resembles a commode that you sit in while warm water circulates around the basin. It's especially soothing for vaginal deliveries and the hemorrhoids you'll most likely get in late pregnancy or during delivery. I highly recommend you make time for one or more sitz baths while you're in the hospital. It's one of those things I wish I'd been able to take home with me from the hospital along with my precious newborn.

POSTPARTUM DEPRESSION

"Baby Blues," or postpartum blues, is used to describe the mild and temporary forms of depression which are quite common during the first weeks after a woman delivers her baby. Typically, this condition appears one to three days after the baby's birth and is characterized by emotional instability, feelings of sadness, prolonged crying, irritability, poor sleep, mood changes and a sense of vulnerability, and can occur anytime during early postpartum. In most cases, it lasts only a few days to a few weeks.

In its more serious form postpartum depression is a dull, gray numbness that can drain the joy and pleasure out of life. In its mildest form, this disorder is a nuisance that interferes with the steady transition into life with a newborn. In extreme cases, it can be a life-threatening situation for either a new mother or her infant.

Depression is a debilitating medical condition that can destroy a mother's ability to think clearly and cope with the everyday responsibilities that come with having a new baby. If you (or your partner) suspect that you suffer from stress or mood swings that are more than those typically associated with the common postpartum experience of raging hormones, seek professional medical help from someone who is experienced with postpartum depression.

Postpartum depression is real—symptoms can be quite subtle in the beginning, but they can intensify rapidly. It can strike any woman regardless of her physiological, economic, or social circumstances. In severe cases, postpartum depression can incapacitate a woman, suspending her ability to care for herself and her newborn.

In a worst case scenario, a woman suffering from extreme postpartum depression is capable of taking her own life or her infant's. Tragically, from time to time we hear about one of these disastrous stories. Please note that depression tends to travel in families, so it's prudent to find out if a parent or grandparent in your family has suffered from depression. The risk of depression triples for children of depressed parents. If someone in your family is depressed, you have a 25 percent greater chance of becoming depressed than if there were no depression in your family.

Depression affects women of all ages, but is most common during the childbearing years. The good news is that depression is remarkably treatable, and in many cases patients enjoy a complete recovery. Postpartum depression affects approximately 10 percent of women. Unfortunately, too many of these women are too embarrassed or uninformed to get the help they need. Consequently, they miss the joy and satisfaction and delight during the early months of motherhood.

> A woman experiencing depression is not alone,
> not to blame, and will be well again!

Depression is no longer a thing to be embarrassed about or hidden. A woman experiencing depression is not alone, not to blame, and will be well again! It's vital that we be honest with ourselves and speak candidly and openly with our family and doctors.

There are many symptoms of depression. I'm listing the common ones for those who may benefit dramatically from knowing what these symptoms are and, in turn, get the help they need.

WARNING SIGNS OF DEPRESSION

- Persistent sad, anxious, empty, or flat mood

- Feelings of helplessness and a low sense of one's own worth

- Lack of interest in things that used to seem fun and exciting

- Sudden change in sleep habits, such as trouble getting to sleep or sleeping too much

- Dramatic weight loss or gain

- Decreased energy, fatigue, feeling slowed down or tired all the time

- Constant feelings of restlessness and irritability

- Difficulty concentrating, remembering things, making decisions, and focusing on tasks

- Thoughts of death or suicide

The following story is a case history of one woman's struggle with severe postpartum depression—it's my story. It tells of both chemical depression and two unusually difficult pregnancies. I include it here for those any woman who may experience either of these conditions and to offer guidance and encouragement for seeking treatment. Although it feels like it, you're not alone and there is relief available.

MICHELLE'S STORY

From the outside looking in, I had an ideal life—a beautiful, healthy, new baby, a loving husband, supportive family and friends, and no significant financial problems. Yet, within a few weeks after the birth of my first child, I was having feelings of helplessness, pessimism, guilt, and worthlessness. I lost interest in things I had previously found pleasurable, like shopping, sports, and sex. I experienced significant weight loss, a dramatic decrease in energy, and I was constantly exhausted no matter how much rest I got. I was unaware that I was experiencing the classic symptoms of depression.

When my first child was about six months old, I finally sought the help of a therapist. This helped to resolve some of my previously existing issues, but it didn't give me the medical help I desperately needed. My undiagnosed misery was beginning to damage my marriage and I was having suicidal thoughts. This went on for more than a year before I bounced back and began to have more energy and a more optimistic feeling about life overall. It was about the time this fog lifted that my husband and I decided to try to have another baby.

This was not a simple decision to make because my first pregnancy was a nightmare—not an average, healthy pregnancy, to say the least. My body reacted as if it were allergic to being pregnant. Within six weeks of conception, I was vomiting constantly, suffering from severe dehydration, and my weight went from 110 to 98 pounds. At around five months pregnant, I was diagnosed with a heart condition, and at seven months I was hospitalized for pre-term labor. The doctors had given us 50/50 odds of having the same kind of experience with any future pregnancy. And here we were, contemplating having another child and hoping to be in the healthy 50 percent this second time around.

I became pregnant with our second child just a few months after escaping the previous period of depression. We were delighted to be pregnant, but unfortunately it was a repeat performance. To our great disappointment, once again we were in the undesirable 50 percent category.

The entire second pregnancy was an ordeal from beginning to end, including countless days of vomiting, incessant trips to the doctor, and two hospitalizations. I was unable to care for myself or our two-year-old daughter. I needed full-time help just to get through a day. My mother came to our rescue, serving as our live-in nanny and housekeeper for five months. Something positive that came out of our difficulties was a fabulous bonding experience for my daughter and her grandmother, and my mom was able to avoid an arctic winter in South Dakota.

We were elated to welcome our son, Samuel, and be finished with our last pregnancy! After he was born, the first two weeks were the usual blend of euphoria and exhaustion. But by the third and fourth weeks, I was crying constantly—usually about nothing. I experienced difficulty concentrating, remembering things, and making simple decisions. I frequently found myself standing in front of an open refrigerator, unable to decide what to eat. More often than not, my indecision meant I simply didn't eat.

Family and friends made gracious offers to help in many ways, but things weren't getting any better. When Sam was a month old, I packed up the two children and myself and flew home to South Dakota to stay with my parents. I was hoping that some extra help and rest would turn things around. Although it was tremendously helpful, it didn't deal with my real problem—chemical depression.

Upon returning home, a close friend took me to lunch and shared some literature on postpartum depression and encouraged me to check out a local support group. Although I read the information and could clearly see the symptoms and patterns in my own life, I was afraid to seek further help. It took another week or so before my misery overcame my fears and I took the necessary steps to get help.

Initially, I went to the local postpartum support group. The woman who directed the program was well acquainted with depression and the problems that face women with newborns and postpartum depression. In a kind and informal way, she asked the right questions and listened carefully. She encouraged me to see a physician and consider medication as a treatment.

Next, I saw my ob-gyn, a wonderful doctor who had seen me through those two nightmare pregnancies. I told him I was having a difficult time coping and thought I might be suffering from postpartum depression. He was not quick to concur with my diagnosis. He recommended blood tests to rule out thyroid problems, which can cause similar symptoms to depression. He said I could be on the fringes of depression, but he certainly didn't think it was severe. In retrospect, clearly I was not candid enough with him regarding my degree of distress.

I felt alone and empty. I was convinced that I was failing miserably as a wife and mother. My feelings were distorting my ability to think rationally, and I was beginning to think that my family would be better of if I weren't around. I wanted to run away. Suicidal thoughts were back again. I'd hit rock bottom and I knew I desperately needed medical help.

Finally, I made an appointment with a psychiatrist who worked with postpartum depression cases. He quickly recognized the signs of depression and discussed three aspects of treatment with me—psychological, social, and biological. After reviewing my case history, he decided that my condition was biologically based and would require medication. What a relief I felt! I thought to myself, Maybe I wasn't just inadequate after all.

The first medication he prescribed produced significant improvement, but was quickly followed by side effects of insomnia, loss of appetite, and strange dreams. Within a few days, I knew I would have to try a different medication, which I did. After that, I experienced further improvement, and with some trial and error we eventually found a medication combination that worked for my highly sensitive system.

It wasn't long before a friend commented that she hadn't seen me in such good spirits in years. Through perseverance I was finally back to being the person I once knew. She had been gone far too long.

One of the most gratifying moments of writing this book occurred when I received a phone call from a woman in Colorado who had been given a copy of my manuscript as a shower gift. At the time, her baby was about nine weeks old. She was quite certain that she was experiencing Postpartum Depression and she desperately wanted help.

Calling me, a total stranger, to ask for help and direction was an incredibly brave thing for her to do. Fortunately, I was able to refer her to Postpartum Support, International (PSI) in Colorado. Better yet, a therapist affiliated with PSI was on her insurance plan and she was able to get the help she needed to regain her health and happiness.

It was an honor and privilege to be a link in this process. My greatest hope for writing this book has been that in some small way it would be an instrument of encouragement and support to other new parents. I am grateful that by sharing my own lamentable story, someone else has benefited.

Postpartum depression affects the entire family unit. Fathers also suffer when a new mother is experiences depression. The most typical responses by new fathers confronted by this are that of fear and confusion. Partners of depressed mothers report the following symptoms:

- Loss of sleep

- Fatigue

- Less freedom

- Increased work

- Performance anxiety

- Increased responsibility

- A decrease in the attention they receive

- Limited support from colleagues

The following story reflects the experience of many men whose partners suffered Post Partum Depression.

Where Did My Wife Go?

My wife and I were ecstatic about the arrival of our first child. We had mindfully prepared for this exciting event for months. What we hadn't prepared for was the possibility that my wife could become so depressed that it would cause her to become dysfunctional as a mother and unavailable to me as a partner and friend.

The challenges that I had to face were inconceivable at the time because I was totally unaware of postpartum depression. When my wife began to experience the first symptoms, I had no idea what was happening and reacted badly. I became angry and frustrated. I was embarrassed and couldn't bring myself to ask for help from family or friends. I thought my wife should just get a grip—pull herself together. I wanted it to go away, but it didn't.

Most confusing for me was the fact that there didn't seem to anything that had precipitated her constant crying, persistent anxiety, insomnia, and the irritability that was often directed at me. I tried not to take her criticisms personally, but we often ended up arguing about trivial matters. As much as I tried to help, she seemed to resent my good intentions and attempts to encourage her. I began to feel more and more pressure to make up for my wife's inability to care for our newborn. My work was suffering and I had stopped all of my usual activities like going to the gym and meeting friends. I felt alone and helpless.

The final straw came when my wife announced she no longer wanted to breast feed or hold the baby. Out of sheer desperation, I called our family doctor and he referred me to a psychiatrist. This was a difficult step for me to take because of the stigma attached to mental illnesses, but I felt I had nowhere else to go. As it turned out, this is the best step I could have taken.

Ignorance is not bliss when it comes to postpartum depression. The most important tool we as fathers have is knowledge. It is important to seek professional help for treatment of this illness because it IS a treatable medical illness. I finally got my wife back. She got better because of the guidance we received from a professional in the field and from the support of family and friends.

What You Can Do

It is possible to reduce the risk of depression by being aware of the symptoms of depression and by following the subsequent strategies for prevention:

- Understand that the responsibilities of motherhood are learned, and become informed.

- Get plenty of rest!

- Get help from your husband or partner, dependable friends and relatives.

- Spend time with other couples who are experienced with child-bearing.

- Don't overload yourself with unimportant tasks.

- Avoid moving soon after your baby arrives.

- Do not be overly concerned with keeping up appearances.

- Do not take on the responsibility of caring for relatives and others during this time.

- Discuss your plans and worries with your husband, family and experienced friends.

- Don't give up outside interests entirely, simply cut back on the schedule of commitments and responsibilities.

- Locate babysitters before your baby arrives and use them as a mother's helper early on.

The idea that caring for a newborn is instinctual and that with motherhood a woman suddenly possesses unwavering and limitless love is a myth! It is also a myth that the birth of a baby brings with it immediate and complete maternal fulfillment. Parenting is a skill that takes time to master. Unfortunately, most new parents receive little, if any, training and hands-on experience. The following strategies can provide substantial assistance to new parents for the postpartum transition.

- Discuss and define shared responsibilities and roles for practically coping with the parental adjustment.

- Identify and arrange for functional and emotional support for the first few months and beyond.

- Identify and implement routines that reduce circumstantial stress.

- Acknowledge that adding a child to your family will necessitate rearranging some of your existing priorities.

- If possible, spend time with an experienced mother of young children before your baby arrives. Continue to socialize with other mothers after your baby is born.

The Symptoms of Postpartum Depression

Physical symptoms:
> Lack of Sleep
> No Energy
> Food Cravings or Loss of Appetite
> Feeling Tired Even after Sleeping

Mental States:
> Anxiety and Excessive Worry
> Confusion
> Great Concern over Physical Changes
> Confusion and Nervousness
> Feeling, "I'm not myself, this isn't me"
> Sadness
> Feeling Overwhelmed

Behavioral:
> Crying More Than Usual
> Hyperactivity or Excitability
> Over sensitivity
> Feelings Hurt Easily
> Irritability
> Lack of Feeling for the Baby

SUMMARY

 Be informed about the issues and options of pregnancy and delivery. Take a birthing class. Read some good reference books like *Your Pregnancy: Every Woman's Guide* or *What to Expect When You're Expecting.*

 Discuss the topic of pain medication and anesthesia with your doctor and partner several weeks, if not months, before labor begins.

 Although giving birth is a natural experience, be aware that it's a unique experience for each woman. Don't make your delivery a test of womanhood. Medical technology has provided us with numerous methods of effective and safe pain relief. It's possible to have both relief and a safe delivery for you and your baby. The smoother your delivery goes, the sooner you'll be ready to care for your newborn and yourself.

 Try not to be overly disappointed if labor and delivery don't go precisely as you have envisioned. They rarely do.

 If you have questions, concerns, or needs about anything—ASK your medical practitioner! It's vital that you be an active participant in your own delivery. Keep asking until you get the information you need. This becomes essential if your regular doctor isn't available when it comes time for you to deliver. Some obstetricians work on-call rotations. This means that if another doctor is on call, he or she will deliver your baby rather than the doctor you've been seeing for your regular checkups. If you have concerns about this, be sure to talk to your doctor well in advance of your due date. Meet with all the physicians in your physician's call rotation. It'll help reduce your stress considerably if you're comfortable with every doctor who presumably could deliver your newborn.

 Remember, the main objective is the health and safety of you and your baby! When the time comes, be prepared to do whatever is best for both of you.

Things to Take to the Hospital: Mom's List

☐ Bathrobe and slippers (no fancy negligees recommended)

☐ Nightgowns, knee length or shorter, washable and designed for nursing. (or use the gowns provided by the hospital)

☐ Cotton or cotton-lined underpants (choose your most inexpensive ones)

☐ Nursing bras and pads (two bras is a good idea)

☐ Lotion for massaging your back and legs

☐ Glasses or contact lenses and supplies (with any solutions and cases you use)

☐ Toiletries, all your regular items, plus, be sure to include lip balm (hair brush, shampoo, hair dryer, deodorant, toothbrush and paste, skin moisturizers)

☐ Warm socks for cold feet, and slippers

☐ Address book, note pad and pen or pencil

☐ Tape/CD player and music if it helps you relax (optional)

☐ Loose-fitting outfit to wear home from the hospital (early maternity size should do)

☐ Comfy going home clothes and blankets for the baby (season and weather appropriate please)

Things to Take to the Hospital: Dad's List

☐ Insurance card

☐ Plenty of change for vending machine snacks and phone calls (bring your phone credit card if you have one)

☐ List of calls and numbers of friends and relatives

☐ Your favorite sandwich or snacks (optional depending on how you feel about your hospitals food)

☐ Film, camera, video camera if desired (throw in some extra batteries!)

☐ A special gift for Mom (jewelry or flowers is likely to be a big hit!)

☐ A great deal of fortitude!

Self Assessment for Postpartum Depression

Read the following statements and circle the answer that most accurately reflects your current feelings:

1. It feels good to be back to my old self again.
   a. The same as always   0
   b. Not quite the same   1
   c. Definitely not the same   2
   d. Not at all   3

2. I look forward to doing my favorite things.
   a. The same as always   0
   b. Not quite the same   1
   c. Definitely not the same   2
   d. Not at all   3

3. I am able to laugh and see the lighter side of things.
   a. The same as always   0
   b. Not quite the same   1
   c. Definitely not the same   2
   d. Not at all   3

4. I am having trouble sleeping.
   a. I am sleeping the same as always   0
   b. Not quite the same   1
   c. Definitely not the same   2
   d. Not at all   3

5. I have been feeling anxious and worried for no good reason.
   a. Not any more than before   0
   b. Somewhat more than before   1
   c. Definitely more than before   2
   d. I am anxious all the time   3

6. I have felt scared and panicky and don't know why.
   a. Not any more than before   0
   b. Somewhat more than before   1
   c. Definitely more than before   2
   d. I have panic attacks and
      I am scared all the time   3

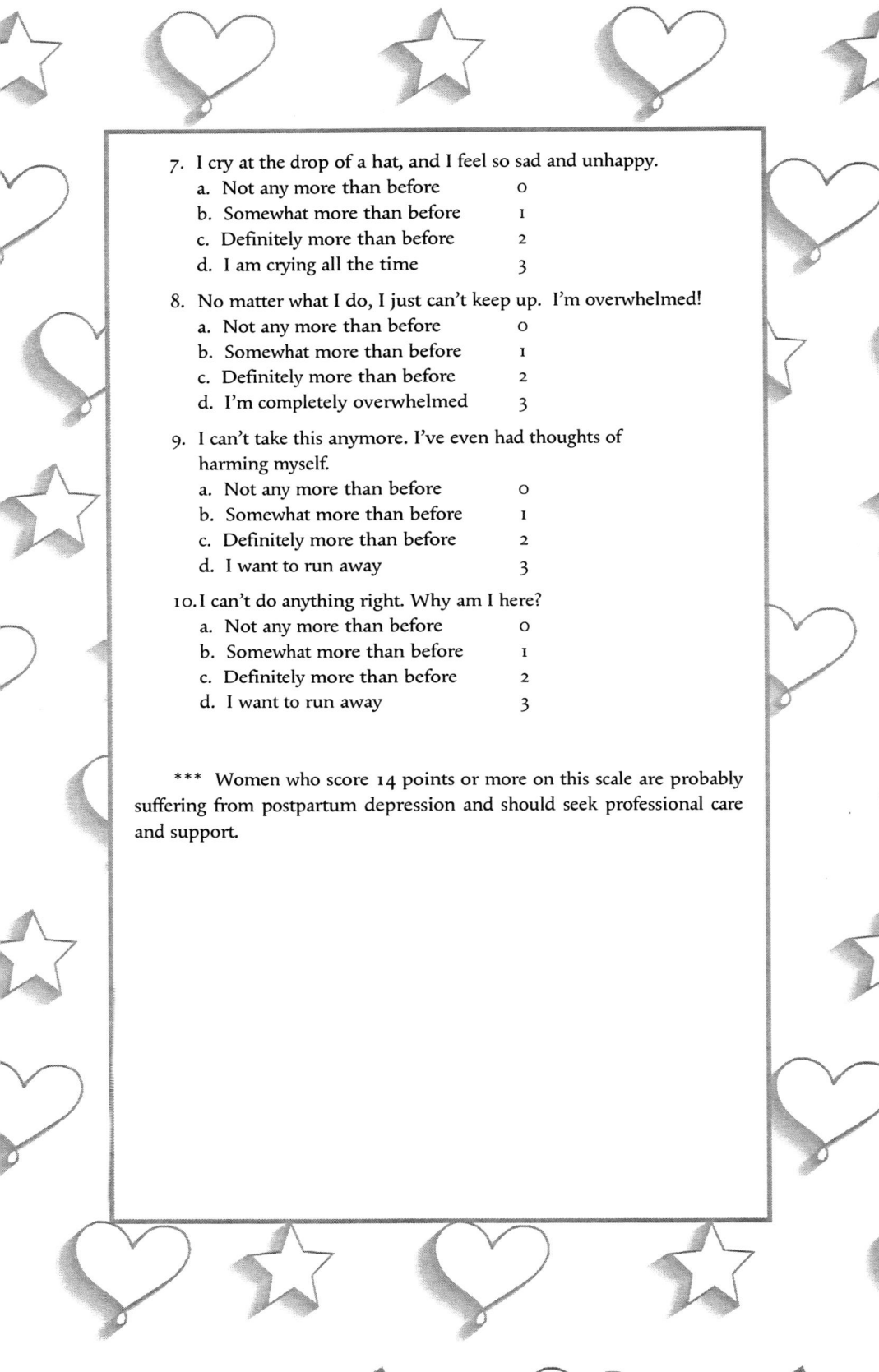

7. I cry at the drop of a hat, and I feel so sad and unhappy.
   a. Not any more than before   0
   b. Somewhat more than before   1
   c. Definitely more than before   2
   d. I am crying all the time   3

8. No matter what I do, I just can't keep up. I'm overwhelmed!
   a. Not any more than before   0
   b. Somewhat more than before   1
   c. Definitely more than before   2
   d. I'm completely overwhelmed   3

9. I can't take this anymore. I've even had thoughts of harming myself.
   a. Not any more than before   0
   b. Somewhat more than before   1
   c. Definitely more than before   2
   d. I want to run away   3

10. I can't do anything right. Why am I here?
    a. Not any more than before   0
    b. Somewhat more than before   1
    c. Definitely more than before   2
    d. I want to run away   3

*** Women who score 14 points or more on this scale are probably suffering from postpartum depression and should seek professional care and support.

Setting Up Camp

Chapter 5

Setting Up Camp

Congratulations! You made it! Now you're at home with your new little bundle of joy. You probably have most of the gear you need in place and are wondering—so what's next?

Setting Up Camp is a process of establishing routines and learning to make use of all the paraphernalia you've just purchased. However, the most important task during this time is getting acquainted with your newborn! Next is learning what makes her happy and determining which cry means she's hungry, tired, or she just needs her mom.

"Magnificent chaos" says it all for about the first ten or twelve weeks—it's truly magnificent and chaotic. All your old routines need to be revised to include your new baby, not to mention figuring out how to make personal time for you and your spouse or partner. If you're lucky, you'll be able to get in some pillow talk before the twelve o'clock midnight feeding. Right now you need to focus on the basic domestic chores and baby care management.

THE HOMECOMING

After packing up the small truckload of paraphernalia we had accumulated at the hospital, we were on our way home—the THREE of us! In our case, it was only a matter of a few blocks, and if it hadn't been for all the extras we had collected, we probably could have put our new daughter in a stroller and walked home. On second thought, Mom (that's me) really needed the ride.

As we arrived at the threshold of our townhouse (not quite like the "just married" threshold when there were only two of us), it became an extended Kodak moment. There were photos to be taken—of Mom and Baby, Grandma and Baby, Baby and Dad, and then, of course, photos of Baby with Mom and Dad. Finally, we were home!

My memories of this first afternoon and evening are somewhat foggy. But then came the moment that I remember most vividly. Paige, our freshly bathed and diapered newborn daughter, was tucked safely into her cradle. My husband and I collapsed into bed and turned out the lights. Then, in the soft glow of nightlight, reality struck us with an overwhelming silence—we were flying solo! At precisely the same moment, Mark and I realized that there was no longer a hospital nursery or baby nurse just down the hall to take care of everything. We were now truly parents.

HOME SWEET HOME

Once you arrive home from the hospital, my advice is to spend at least the first forty-eight hours snuggling and cuddling with your baby and doing only what absolutely needs to be done. This means eating, sleeping, changing diapers, sleeping, soaking in a warm tub, sleeping, and otherwise enjoying and getting to know your new baby. This goes for Dad, too! If everyone is feeling up to it, and weather permits, a short stroll can be revitalizing.

You may be tempted to call all of your closest friends and relatives to come for a viewing of your newest creation, but don't do it! If the urge strikes, review the Ten Commandments for the Postpartum Mother on page 89. Then make yourselves some tea and curl up in a comfy spot. This kind of routine should continue until Mom is well on the road to recovery. After this, you can start dealing with everyday life again and visitors.

During the first six to twelve weeks, most babies are content to sit in their infant seat or car seat, provided they're fed and dry. Take advantage of this time and go out for a simple dinner or take in a movie. Just remember to bring along a light blanket that you can drape over the handle of the carrier so your baby isn't exposed to unwanted elements like drafts and other people's germs.

PHOTO OPPORTUNITIES

Perhaps you're already a shutter bug and delight in being an amateur photographer, or maybe you're simply inclined to record any special event on film. Whatever the case, the birth of a child is an excellent incentive for taking plenty of pictures. Video and still shots are both wonderful and will provide you with memories to cherish for years to come.

It's a good idea to check out your equipment, or acquire some, well in advance of your baby's arrival so you'll be familiar with how to operate it. Starting early also gives you the opportunity to watch for sales on film, batteries, and other pieces of equipment such as lenses.

Some people like to photograph the entire delivery of their baby. This is an extremely personal choice that couples must make individually. What is most important is to clearly let your wishes be known to each other and the delivery staff well in advance. You won't be thinking about what pictures to take or who should take them when delivery time comes.

One option is to have a family member or close friend as the designated photographer. During times when you may not want others in the delivery room with you, one of the nurses may be happy to point and shoot. Just don't expect award-winning photos from any such draftees!

If you like the idea of making photo albums and photo scrapbooks, put these items on your shower wish list. Protective photo box-type files are popular, also a great shower gift, and they're a good way to protect photos and negatives—at least until you have a chance to frame your photos or put them into albums.

Here's a list of suggested shots you won't want to miss:

- Mom and Dad together soon after you find out you're expecting
- A profile shot of Mom shortly before delivery (birthday suit optional)
- Your newborn as soon after delivery as possible
- Your newborn being weighed for the first time
- Mom and the baby as soon as both are ready
- A family picture as soon as the three of you are together
- A group family picture along with the doctor and primary nurse(s) who were with you during labor and delivery
- Mom and the baby leaving the hospital
- The new family upon arriving home
- Various shots of family and friends with the baby
- Your newborn the bassinet or cradle, both sleeping and awake
- Your new infant on the changing table getting diapers changed
- Various shots of Mom and Dad snuggling the baby in their arms, holding the baby while she or he is sleeping, and sitting in the rocking chair together.
- Numerous shots of a happy baby (or a crying baby) in his or her favorite places like the swing or bouncie chair

- Baby and the household pets

- Your newborn during events such as religious ceremonies

- Your newborn wearing some of her or his special outfits

- Baby surrounded by stuffed animals and other special gifts

You'll no doubt take an excessive amount of photos of your newborn, but it's better to have too many than not enough. Experiment and take plenty of candid shots—sometimes they end up being your favorites. Black and white photos are always a good addition to your collection. Click away! And be sure to get double prints so you can share the memories with grandparents and your siblings—many photo stores have special rates for the second set of prints.

MANAGING THE MAGNIFICENT CHAOS

Couples deal with adding a baby to their lives in many different ways. In the long run, extremes of any kind can be detrimental to the success in establishing a healthy daily relationship with your newborn. Some couples become completely subordinate to the needs and whims of their baby to the exclusion of their own. Others carry on with their pre-parenthood routines with too little regard for the changes required to fulfill their newborn's fundamental necessities.

Parents and new babies essentially have the same basic needs for food, rest, safety, and love. A reasonable goal for the first few weeks is to try to develop a routine that provides each of you with an adequate supply of these basics. Accomplishing this requires some planning, open and honest communication, and teamwork.

Unfortunately, parenting is not an innate skill. But you can learn. Naturally, if you've had much younger siblings or extensive baby-sitting experience, you may already know how to care for a seven- or eight-pound new baby. If not, don't expect immediate perfection from yourself or your mate. Putting the diaper on backwards or being a little awkward when rocking a wailing newborn in your arms is not a serious problem. Be supportive of each other and the ways in which you individually relate to your new little one and the rest will come with time.

Without even realizing it, most of the daily chores in your life will take on a completely different nature. Here's a list of tasks and issues, some of which you'll be confronting for the first time, that may require a new approach.

Grocery shopping and errands. Your first decision may be whether to shop with or without your baby. Without requires planning ahead for a time when your partner or a baby-sitter can stay with your infant. Generally speaking, departing as soon as your baby goes down for a nap is a good plan. This reduces the anxiety you may feel about leaving your newborn, especially in the first couple of weeks.

If you do take your baby with you when you go shopping, nap time departure is still a good idea. Oftentimes a car ride will lull your baby to sleep, and you can simply place the car seat in the grocery cart. Many stores have carts designed to accommodate car seats. Make sure you place the car seat in a secure position, whether you attach it to the rails of the cart or place it in the large basket area of the cart. This will limit the volume of groceries that will fit, so you may want to do your major shopping without the baby in tow.

Laundry. Your baby may only be six or seven pounds at birth, but the amount of laundry that piles up quickly with this tiny addition to your family is amazing. On a good day, your baby can easily go through two or three outfits, not to mention several burp towels, linens, and blankets. If you have laundry facilities in your home, plan to throw in a couple of loads each day. If you must go out to a community laundry room or Laundromat, plan your outing in much the same way as described above for grocery shopping.

The key to success here is to get together everything you need before you leave the house. This includes items such as bleach and fabric softener. If you forget something, it's more than annoying to have to go back for it. A well-stocked diaper bag is also essential! You might want to throw in a book or a couple of magazines to read if your baby falls asleep while you're doing the laundry. (It's a nice thought, but I'm not sure if it ever actually happens!)

Taking walks. As soon as your recovery permits, putting your baby in a stroller and taking a walk is a great way to get some mild exercise and fresh air. Naturally, the safety of your baby is your first consideration. Avoid streets where there's a lot of traffic and no sidewalks. A busy bike path is not a good match for a stroller either. If you're walking your dog along with your baby, your pet's leash manners or willingness to follow where you go will determine the success of this type of outing. When you begin taking walks, with or without a dog, stay close to home or near your parked car in the event that one of you (Baby, Dog, or Mom) finds the walk less than pleasurable.

Meeting friends. Meeting a friend for lunch or coffee often becomes a new mom's favorite activity. And why not? It's a very pleasant reward after all the work and changes you've been through to have friends and other moms fawning and cooing over your newborn.

As mentioned earlier, going out should not pose a problem in the early weeks provided that the location you've chosen has room for an infant car seat or stroller. When the weather is good, I highly recommend outdoor cafes or restaurants with patios. Places that have a reasonable level of background noise can help lull your baby to sleep. It also helps to muffle any baby in distress noises that might arise.

Feeding your baby on the go. Whether you're nursing exclusively, using a bottle, or both, sooner or later there will be a time when you'll need to feed your baby away from home. As with all the other baby activities, planning ahead will significantly reduce the stress and increase your enjoyment while accomplishing the task.

If you're a nursing mother, wear something comfortable that allows you to nurse without undressing. If you're new at it, select a location that grants you the comfort and privacy you desire. Many department stores now have sections in their restroom lounges where moms can nurse. Your car or a quiet park bench can also be conducive for feeding a baby. In a pinch, a blanket over the shoulder can provide adequate privacy almost anywhere.

> *I can hardly believe some of the places I've nursed our children. On one occasion I found myself sitting sideways on a toilet in the ladies room at the Metrodome football stadium. Why you ask? Well, I wasn't quite comfortable with the idea of nursing our one-month-old baby in the stands with forty thousand other spectators.*

Diaper bags: The baby's survival kit! Each outing with your little one in tow will require putting together the following essentials before leaving the house: a car seat, stroller or baby pack, and a diaper bag. Some parents have two bags—a smaller one with minimum items for short outings, and a larger everything bag for day trips or an occasional overnight. The smaller diaper bag generally carries one to two diapers, travel-size wipes, and barrier cream, a plastic bag, burp cloth, pacifier, and bottle. If you're breast-feeding, the bottle can be a small one that you put water in if you end up having to stretch the baby's feeding time.

Although the designs of diaper bags are as varied as their owners, the contents are fairly standard in the everything bag. Here are the basics:

As you become more familiar with your baby's personal needs, you'll be able to customize the contents of the diaper bag to fit both your and the baby's needs.

- Diapers

- Diaper wipes

- Changing pad or large lap pad

- Barrier cream

- Small plastic bags

- One to two servings of formula

- Bottled water

- Burping cloth or extra cloth diaper

- Change of clothes for the baby

- Sunscreen

- Extra blanket and/or sweater

- Pacifier

- Toys or visual stimulant for infants

- Snack for Mom

- Money: a couple of dollars and change for little emergencies.

Pets and a new baby. With some thought and planning, most pets can coexist happily with a baby. However, the baby's safety must always take precedence and you must be prepared to confine or remove the pet from your home if it becomes a health or safety risk to your child.

Whatever pets you may have around your home, the big issues are their temperament, size, and energy level. All these things will have an impact on their compatibility with your baby. If you own a large, frisky canine, for example, you may need a place like a garage or dog run where your pet can be confined. Initially, the concern is to keep the pet from nose-to-nose contact with your baby. As your child grows older, interaction will increase and pets and children usually will become best friends.

Allergies are another concern. In most cases, if neither you nor your partner is allergic to pets of any kind, then your baby is less likely to be allergic. Still, be sure to let your pediatrician know what pets are in your home. If you're anxious about disease or other health issues, consult a veterinarian as well as your pediatrician.

Baby's naptime. Naptime varies widely from infant to infant. Napping at home, snuggled in their own cradle or crib, is great, but if you're an on the go mom, your baby will have to learn to nap in a car seat, at other people's homes, and in your arms—wherever they may be.

Experience teaches that flexibility and sensitivity are both important factors when it comes to nap times for any child. Before your baby is finished taking naps, they'll go through many phases of sleeping needs. I believe it's good to have a basic routine, but don't become too rigid about how and when your baby naps—you'll all be happier if you stay loose in the saddle.

Where baby sleeps. There are many theories about where a baby should sleep—a bassinet, a cradle, in the parents' room, in the parents' bed. I'm convinced that the best place for your baby to sleep is wherever the entire family will get the most rest.

During the first few weeks, particularly if you're nursing, having the baby in your room is the most convenient option. It's also reassuring to be able to hear your baby breathing and moving in the night. However, if either partner is an especially light sleeper, having your infant in the room could be a problem. Babies frequently make little grunts and other noises that can wake one or both parents and thus interrupt their much needed rest. In this situation, once you're more confident with the nighttime routine, having your baby sleep in their own room does have its rewards.

When your baby is fussy or otherwise in distress, snuggling with her in your bed can be a quick solution. Be forewarned, however, that this may become your baby's favorite place to sleep, and pediatricians recommend against establishing this habit. For the most part, trial and error will be your best bet. Especially in the first few months, your baby's sleeping habits will change frequently, so be flexible and prepared to change along with her.

Communicating with your baby. Communication is a delicate mix of touch, sound, smell, and sight. Talking to your infant is just one of the ways you communicate. Generally speaking, babies tend to respond more favorably to higher pitched voices. They love to see your smile, and your energy level influences their responses. For feeding and sleep time, quieter and more soothing expressions and sounds are more appropriate.

All the research coming out now about child development clearly describes babies as little sponges, soaking up the stimuli around from the time they're born. This is contrary to past beliefs that babies are simply hungry little blobs for the first couple of years. Based on the new information, it seems only right to speak to your baby as you would any other person. Your child will clearly understand your message long before he or she responds with words.

SUPPORT GROUPS AND ENCOURAGEMENT

I can't overemphasize the value of support and encouragement during the transition period and throughout the parenting experience. Regardless of your personal style of parenting and general lifestyle, having a network of support people and services will make the adventure into parenthood a far more pleasurable one.

There are many ways to get support and, in turn, be supportive. If you're already part of a circle of friends who have young children, you'll get a lot of help and advice there. If you don't have friends with children, don't worry, because you probably will soon. It comes with the territory, so to speak—the territory being the parks and playgrounds in your area where you'll take your baby on outings and gather with some hopefully like-minded moms. It's reassuring to spend time with other new parents from diverse backgrounds and find out that they're facing many of the same issues as you. After all, the parenting adventure is a universal one.

If you have a network previously established or you live near your parents or other close relatives, you may not need a more

formal support group like PEP (Parents Education Program) or
MOPS (Moms of Pre-schoolers). Keep in mind, though, there are
many groups like this available to you. (See the appendix for a
listing.) Occasionally, you may find it refreshing and beneficial to
get some objective feedback from outside your immediate circle of
family and friends. Plus, an extra pat on the back never hurts,
especially when you're feeling the need for one.

MAKING YOUR HOME SAFE AND APPROPRIATE FOR A CHILD

I'm not sure where the term "childproofing" comes from, or
why it caught on the way it did. I find it to be a confusing term-is
it like waterproofing? If something is waterproof, it keeps water
out. If something is childproof, then it follows that it keeps a child
out. I thought the whole idea was to bring a child into the home,
not to keep them out. I'm uncomfortable with the term, not the
idea behind it. I prefer to think of childproofing as "child safety"
and "child appropriate."

Safety issues in the home must be taken seriously. Electrical
outlets and cords should be covered—and minimized, if possible.
Make sure you have smoke and carbon monoxide detectors
installed and in good working order. Test them regularly.

Furniture with sharp edges can cause injury to toddlers who
are just beginning to explore their surroundings. Corner guards
and bumpers for coffee tables and dining tables are on the market.
Breakable items and things small enough to be swallowed must be
put in places that are unreachable for a child. Move all cleaning
supplies, pesticides, and other caustic materials to overhead
cabinets. The less accessible these items are, the safer your child
will be and the more peace of mind you'll have.

Close supervision is always the best safety measure you can
take, but it's wise to survey your home in regard to everything
that's waist level and below. Any item that can burn, cut, poke,
scratch, pinch, or poison your child must be modified or removed.

Some couples find that latches for cupboards and drawers are helpful for a short period of time.

This is not the time in your life to be excessively concerned with your home's decor. Safety and functionality are paramount. There will be plenty of time later when your child is older to focus on the interior aesthetics of your home.

PRE-KID ENVIRONMENT VS. CHILD IN THE HOME

Pre-kid homes have light-colored walls and carpets. Furniture, artwork, and china displays with aesthetics and design in mind are the objectives. Post-kid homes are by nature required to be different. You need washable walls and floors, trash cans with lids, and only articles that can be easily replaced. In other words, set things up so you don't have to take out a new home equity loan every year for repairs and repainting.

If you have adequate living space, designate a kid room. This area is the exclusive domain of toys and turmoil. By doing this, it establishes a message for both parents and kids about what activities take place in which parts of your home. It's especially convenient when other toddlers visit and even more helpful when you need to do a fast shovel and shut for unexpected company.

Making a home appropriate for a child refers to things like sturdy furniture that can endure and support a toddler's unsteady balance and resist various bodily fluids. It also applies to toys and equipment that are age and size appropriate. Naturally, all of these considerations change as your child grows and acquires new levels of curiosity and mobility.

Excellent parenting, like so much of what is covered in this book, is a lifestyle choice that encompasses many responsibilities. It's never too early to develop a mentality that always puts your child's health and safety first.

SUMMARY

 It's just a matter of time before you'll begin to settle into new routines and engage in new activities. The best advice I can give you about setting up camp is to think carefully about the way you'd like your daily life to run—the feel of it. Do you prefer structure in your life or do you enjoy a lot of spontaneity? What causes you to stress out? What helps you relax and enjoy life?

 If the old saying "How you spend your time is how you'll spend your life" is true, then it's important to put some effort into organizing your time in ways that meet your needs for a healthy environment overall. To be sure, there will be sleepless nights and some difficult moments that seem eternal, but you'll be amazed at how quickly the weeks and months fly by. Before you know it, you'll be planning your child's first birthday party.

Exploring Child Care

Chapter 6

Exploring Child Care

One of the most daunting tasks faced by new parents is making arrangements for child care. This applies to everyone, regardless of who they are, where they live, how they're employed, or their economic status. As parents, whether your need is for an occasional sitter or full-time child care, the fears and concerns are the same. We all want our children to be in the care of someone who is committed to their well-being.

If you're returning to work within three months or less after your baby's arrival, it's essential that you select and reserve child care well in advance of your child's birth. As you begin to explore the options, you may find that your choices are narrowed because of cost or availability.

Regardless of the unique circumstances that influence your decision, always listen to your intuition. If you feel the slightest doubt about a person or place, then move on to the next choice. In the end, perseverance will pay off with your peace of mind. The time you spend networking with other parents and exploring your child care options is a priceless investment in your family.

TIMING IS EVERYTHING!

Five days after my first child was born, I received two offers to buy my business—the three hair salons I had been operating for over seven years. Suddenly, I was faced with learning to care for a newborn, negotiating the sale of my company, and becoming a stay-at-home mom all at once. Unfortunately, what I didn't understand at the time was that I should have arranged for child care before the baby arrived.

In a panic, I solicited the help of a cherished friend who had two children of her own. She watched my newborn for three or four hours a day, three times a week, while I sorted things out with my business. Naturally, this situation didn't last forever, but it did provide me with the opportunity to focus on selling my business and to investigate other child care options.

After several temporary child care situations, I found a highly capable young woman to come into my home three times a week. She began working with us when my daughter, Paige, was six months old. I can't overemphasize the importance of doing your child care homework long before your baby arrives. Thank goodness I didn't have to return to work six or twelve weeks after Paige's birth. I didn't have child care arrangements in place and I don't know what I would have done without my friend's help.

WHAT'S OUT THERE?

There are two aspects of child care that must be carefully locked at: your needs and preferences and the child care options available in your area. Begin by envisioning what quality child care is and what your ideal situation would be, regardless of cost.

When you can answer the following questions, you've established a foundation for beginning your child care search. The answers to these questions will help you identify and select a care situation that meets your family's individual needs and conditions.

- Do you want your child cared for in your home or outside your home?

- Do you need full-time, part-time or extended help? How many hours per week: ten, twenty-five, or fifty?

- Do you want live-in help? Do you have adequate space and privacy for a live-in caretaker?

- What is your child care budget? How flexible is your budget?

As you begin to think about what quality child care is, I encourage you to place the emphasis on the caregivers/staff first and the facility second. I'll say more about inspecting a facility later. When evaluating the staff, here are some considerations:

- Do you get a sense that the staff is there because they want to be there, that it's more than just a job to them?

- Do they communicate with the children in a way that's appropriate to their age?

- Do you sense a nurturing tenderness in the way the caregivers attend to the children?

- How are the people skills in general of the staff? Can they interact comfortably and communicate effectively with the parents (you) as well as the children?

The best child care programs involve and support parents and their children. They may include parent discussion groups, educational events, and resource materials. If you find a place that has these items, you've found a great place to care for your child when you can't be with her!

IN-HOME CHILD CARE

Typically, there are two types of in-home child care—live-in or day care. If you select a live-in nanny or au pair, you'll compensate them with room and board and a small salary. The additional monetary compensation depends on the total number of hours they'll be working.

For example, 35 hours x $6.50 = $227.50/week x 52 weeks 12 months = $986/month. Check your local newspaper's classified section for rates on private room rentals that include bath and kitchen privileges. This will help you determine the value of room and board in your area. Subtract this amount from the total compensation to determine the salary due. Based on the above example, room and board per month would be $500.00 and the salary would be $486.00 per month.

In-home day care providers include family, friends, college students, or other individuals willing to come into your home and care for your child for as few or as many hours per week as needed. This kind of child care tends to be more available and affordable in most areas of the country. To accommodate a more complex schedule, you may need to hire more than one caregiver. However, I recommend that you limit your primary caregivers to no more than two, especially during the first two years, because continuity and familiarity are important to an infant's sense of security and well-being.

Both of the alternatives mentioned above have advantages and disadvantages and will be influenced by your individual needs, preferences, and geographic location. A live-in caregiver often becomes like part of the family. When the relationship is going well, this can be a wonderful experience. However, if problems arise, it can impact the quality of your child care and vice versa. Live-in arrangements tend to work better when all parties involved have a lot of privacy during nonworking hours. Consider your living quarters carefully when contemplating a live-in caregiver. With either arrangement, I strongly recommend that you have a signed employment agreement between yourself and the caregiver (see the sample forms at the end of this chapter).

OUT-OF-HOME CHILD CARD

The options for out-of-home child care include private home day care (a family member or friend cares for your child in their home) and group day care centers that may be licensed or not. The quality of child care providers varies widely from excellent to appalling. You'll find places that serve small groups of from 3 to 6 children, larger centers that handle 20 to 25 children, and ones that accommodate 150 to 200 children divided into small groups overseen by many staff members.

Ultimately, this is a highly personal choice determined by what's available in your area and your impressions of the home or center when you visit it. As I've said before, each situation has advantages and disadvantages. Once you've determined that a provider is safe and qualified, then you'll just have to choose the one that feels right to you.

COOPERATIVE DAY CARE

Cooperative day care is an alternative that is growing in many communities. This is where a group of mothers join together to care for each other's children a certain number of hours each month. Care may be provided in a center or by rotating from home to home of the co-op members.

CORPORATE DAY CARE

More and more, employers are becoming involved with providing child care for their employees. This happens primarily in three ways: an in-house facility, a nearby facility, or a local child care provider that the company contracts with. In some cases, the cost of child care is subsidized by the employer, making it more economical than other options.

If you work for a company that offers in-house day care, this arrangement can give you extra time with your child at lunchtime and during breaks. It also saves you commuting time when your child goes to the same place that you do. And it can also be comforting to know you're close by should there be an emergency.

MAPPING OUT A PLAN

There are many issues to think about before selecting a child care provider. You could easily miss a good situation or select the wrong caregiver if you're unclear about your personal needs and preferences. If you can effectively communicate your likes and dislikes to potential applicants, you'll have a better chance of creating the most compatible situation for you and your family.

Start by thinking about what's most important to you and your family. Will you need part-time or full-time help? What are your budget requirements? Do you want your child to stay in your home or go out to another location? Would you prefer to have your child alone with the caregiver or with other children?

Is it important to you that the child care provider shares a similar philosophy about the growth and development of children? You may have specific ideas about what should be included in your child's daily activities and what forms of entertainment may be used on a daily basis. Whatever your viewpoints are, it's important to express them clearly and emphatically at the very beginning.

If you're looking for a private care arrangement, especially someone to live in with you and your family, do consider preparing an employment agreement that includes your expectations and guidelines for the caregiver. The more specific this document is, the fewer the problems should be later on. If problems do arise, this document will be invaluable in resolving conflicts or dissolving the employment obligation (see the sample employment agreement at the end of this chapter).

LAUNCHING THE SEARCH

If you'll be needing infant care as soon as four to six weeks after birth, you must start the hunt early. Begin your research a few months before the baby is born. The space in day care centers fills up quickly, and finding a sitter of your choice is time consuming.

Use the networking approach. Your best bet is always a personal referral from someone you respect and trust. If you happen to have a circle of friends who are at various stages of raising families, you have some immediate resources to begin with. Bear in mind, however, that friends are sometimes reluctant to give you names of their favorite sitters for fear of losing one or more of them. Other than contacts from friends, there are several places you can approach for possible child care providers:

- **Local colleges.** Check to see if your local colleges and universities have a job bulletin board or referral service. Childhood development and elementary education majors are good candidates.

- **Athletic clubs frequently have child care programs.** Most of the caregiver positions are part-time and often the staff members are interested in additional hours. This is a good way to test drive the caregivers before hiring them to work for you individually.

- **PEP groups.** These are new mothers' support organizations that can put you in touch with many different individuals who are often excellent referral sources for child care providers of all kinds.

- **Places of worship.** Many religious organizations have bulletin boards you can check out. Some provide or rent space to day care facilities. If your place of worship has an active youth program, you might want to speak with the youth coordinator. He or she may know a couple of high school students who work in the nursery department of the group or do baby-sitting.

- **Senior citizens.** Remember when grandmas used to be a mother's best baby-sitter? It's likely that there are a few older women available in your area who would love to become a surrogate grandparent. Check with some of your local senior citizen organizations for possible referrals.

- **Pediatricians.** Your baby's doctor may have some recommendations. A physician's office often has an information board where notices are put up by prospective caregivers. You may want to post a notice of your own soliciting candidates.

- **Agencies.** Check the yellow pages for referrals. Look under "Child Care" and "Nanny Services." Some agencies specialize in nannies and au pairs, while others handle licensed child-care providers. Referral agencies usually charge a fee, but the applicants are generally professional child care providers. Always follow through with at least two reference checks. Your child's safety and well-being depend on it!

- **Local publications.** The classified section of parenting magazines, newspapers, and other publications in your area may provide a list of nannies and day care centers. Caregivers often place ads in local papers when they're looking for employment.

INSPECTING THE FACILITIES

If you opt for a day care center, it's important to do an in-person evaluation of the premises before you enroll your child. Make several short visits to the facility during various times of the day. This will give you an opportunity to observe the atmosphere of the surroundings while children are playing together, having lunch or snacks, and during their rest period. Meet with the director of each facility you're considering. Discuss the philosophical orientation of the center to determine if their approach is compatible with your own. Consider only child care centers that allow you access to your child at any time, with or without a prescheduled appointment. During your survey, be sure to check out the following details:

- **General appearance.** Is the space orderly or in disarray? Avoid centers that are extreme in either of these appearances. Is it aesthetically child-centered in appearance?

- **Licensed facility.** Licensing governs the safety and cleanliness of a center. Make sure the state license of the center is current and in good standing. The license must be posted in a visible spot. If you don't see it, ask to see it. A license alone doesn't determine the quality of care your child will get, but it's important that the center meets the required minimum standards of the state licensing bureau.

- **Staff ratios.** One caregiver to every four infants is standard. The ratio for toddlers and preschoolers is a bit higher. Spend some time observing how the caregivers interact with the children. Are the children happy? What kinds of activities are they involved in? Centers that have teams who work together with the children may provide better interaction with your child than those who work independently.

- **Experience of staff.** Education and experience are valuable and will influence the care your child receives. However, these credentials alone don't guarantee the perfect caregiver. Attitude is a major factor. Do the caregivers show respect for the children as individuals? Are the children appropriately clean (i.e., noses wiped, food cleaned off their faces, etc.)? How do they respond to children who are sad or angry? Modeling healthy conflict management skills and teaching the children these skills from the beginning is a substantial advantage.

- **Pick-up and drop-off.** What are the security procedures for dropping off and picking up children from the center? Parents must be certain that only the individuals they designate will be allowed to collect their child.

- **Safety.** The general condition of the structures and furnishings should be good. Are the toys age appropriate and cleaned on a regular basis. Any outdoor play equipment should meet regulations. Ask if the staff is trained in CPR and first aid. This is a must. Take note of electrical outlets, doors, windows, smoke detectors, and fire escape routes. What types of locks or latches are used on gates and doors?

- **Food preparation.** If meals are prepared at the center, tour the kitchen. Who prepares the food and where is it prepared? Is the food served family style or in individual portions to the children? Is there adequate refrigeration and sanitary storage?

SUMMARY

 Child care is the most significant single expense new parents incur. If you plan to return to work within six to twelve weeks after your babies arrives, start setting up your day care arrangements three to four months before your due date. The time and energy you invest in this process will be invaluable. It'll mean peace of mind for you and a safe, happy experience for your baby.

 If you're ambivalent about going back to work, you may find significant emotional and financial benefits by spending the first six to twelve months at home with your baby. When considering this question, compare the total cost of child care and other expenses such as clothes for work, transportation, parking, and so forth with your take-home pay. Some women find that by economizing and reorganizing their discretionary spending, they're better off financially and emotionally staying at home with their new baby.

 First-time mothers who have made a career for themselves are often determined to return to their jobs after a few weeks at home with their newborn. This works for many women; however, when actually faced with leaving their child every day, some women change their mind. If this happens to you, don't beat yourself up about it; relax and enjoy the experience of taking care of your baby yourself. Babies grow up all too quickly, and there's no better child care than a loving, enthusiastic new mother. By the time your baby is six, twelve, or eighteen months old, you may be ready to go back to work, and your baby may be ready for some social stimulation in a daycare setting.

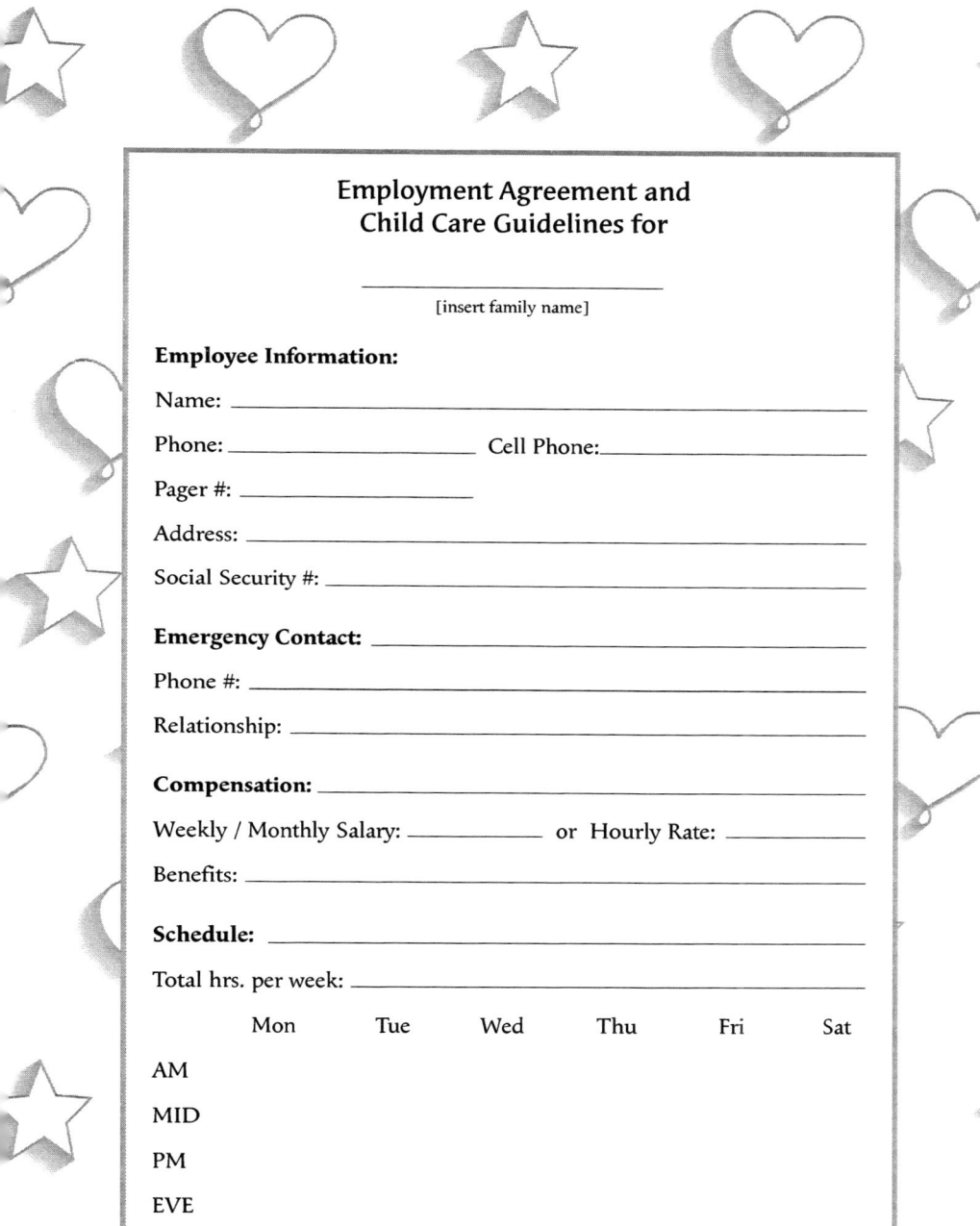

Employment Agreement and
Child Care Guidelines for

_____
[insert family name]

Employee Information:

Name: _____

Phone: _____ Cell Phone: _____

Pager #: _____

Address: _____

Social Security #: _____

Emergency Contact: _____

Phone #: _____

Relationship: _____

Compensation: _____

Weekly / Monthly Salary: _____ or Hourly Rate: _____

Benefits: _____

Schedule: _____

Total hrs. per week: _____

	Mon	Tue	Wed	Thu	Fri	Sat
AM						
MID						
PM						
EVE						
NIGHT						

I accept and agree to the preceding employment conditions and will adhere to the job description and guidelines attached.

Signed: _____ Date: _____

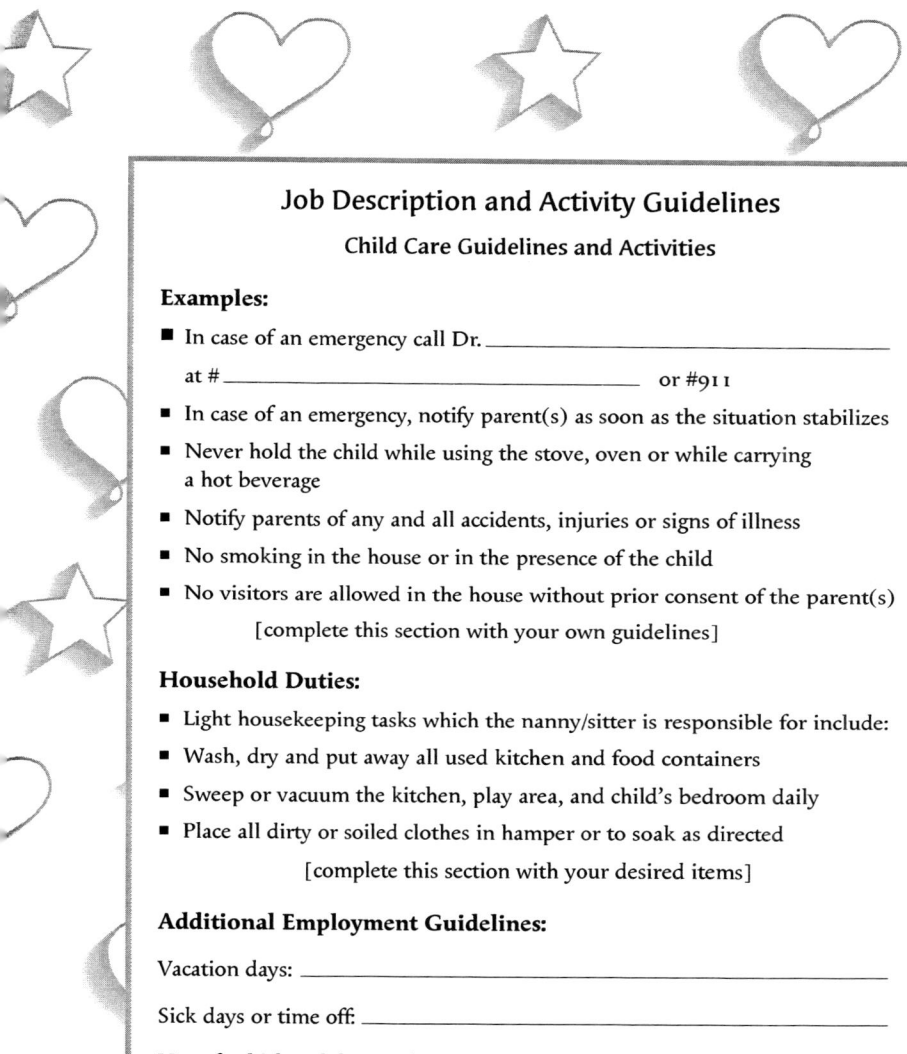

Job Description and Activity Guidelines

Child Care Guidelines and Activities

Examples:

- In case of an emergency call Dr. _____
  at # _____ or #911
- In case of an emergency, notify parent(s) as soon as the situation stabilizes
- Never hold the child while using the stove, oven or while carrying a hot beverage
- Notify parents of any and all accidents, injuries or signs of illness
- No smoking in the house or in the presence of the child
- No visitors are allowed in the house without prior consent of the parent(s)

    [complete this section with your own guidelines]

Household Duties:

- Light housekeeping tasks which the nanny/sitter is responsible for include:
- Wash, dry and put away all used kitchen and food containers
- Sweep or vacuum the kitchen, play area, and child's bedroom daily
- Place all dirty or soiled clothes in hamper or to soak as directed

    [complete this section with your desired items]

Additional Employment Guidelines:

Vacation days: _____

Sick days or time off: _____

Use of vehicles, clubs or other amenities: _____

Additions and Changes:

_____

_____

_____

Signed: _____ Dated: _____

Signed: _____ Dated: _____

Household Information Form

Emergency Phone Numbers:

Residence Location:
    Family Name:
    Address:
    Phone:
    Directions and Local Landmarks:

Where We Keep Things:
    First Aid Supplies
    Fire Extinguisher
    Flash Lights
    Alarms (fire/security)
    Thermostat
    Fuse Box

In Case of Emergency:

Accident:

Fire:

Earthquake or Natural Disaster:
    What to Do
    Where to Go

Prowler or Unwanted Visitor:

Notes or Comments:

Consulting with Dr. Carole

Chapter 7

Consulting with Dr. Carole

In days gone by, the birth of a child and the care of an infant were collective efforts by an extended family. Mothers and grandmothers, sisters and aunts, passed on the customs of parenting firsthand. In addition to the routine care and feeding, parents were often called upon to fill the role of physician for their ailing child, which generally consisted of limited home remedies, hope, and a lot of wait and see. Although there's something to be said even today for home remedies, I find the guidance of a well-trained medical professional invaluable.

Carole Buchholz, M.D., a certified pediatrician, is our expert medical consultant for this chapter. Equally important as her medical training is her experience as a mother of two. She shares with us some essentials for getting smoothly through the early weeks of your newborn's life.

First Dr. Carole shares with us what she tells the first-time parents she meets in her practice. Following that is material the American Academy of Pediatrics has written for new parents. These two sections provide vital information on the most common infant health issues that new parents face in the first six to twelve weeks with their newborn.

CHOOSING YOUR BABY'S DOCTOR

Envision your newborn's first visit to the baby doctor—that special person you hope your child will have fond memories of and the individual you'll be entrusting your baby's health issues to.

There are a number of resources for finding your baby's physician. These include the nursing staff in the hospital nursery, teaching hospitals, your local chapter of the American Medical Association, friends who have children, expectant mothers in your childbirth class, or the class teacher.

If you're using an obstetrician, ask them to recommend a couple of pediatricians. Whoever you ask, give them some simple details about your preferences for a baby doctor. Whatever your criteria, the most important thing is that you trust and feel comfortable with your pediatrician. Therefore, you'll want to interview a few candidates before making a final decision. Below are several things to keep in mind during this process:

- **Insurance:** What insurance plan(s) does the physician participate in? It should coincide with yours. What are the limits for out-of-pocket expenses? How much will you pay for prescriptions and co-pays? If you select a pediatrician outside your policy's provider network, how much extra will you need to pay to be able to see this doctor?

- **Preferences:** Pediatricians include men and women who range in age from twenty-nine to seventy-five! They may have their own young children, grown children, or no children at all. They can be married, single, or divorced—just like the rest of us. Do you have a preference for the age, sex, race, or training of your baby's physician? Even if you don't, by the time your child is a couple of years old, they may have an opinion about what doctor they want to see.

- **Office:** What types of office settings do you like? Do you prefer a cozy atmosphere or are you comfortable with a more functional, clinical environment? A stunning decor is nice, but who pays for it? Probably you will. Does the office handle insurance forms? What kind(s) of payment does the office accept (do they accept cash, checks, credit cards, or payment terms)?

Start getting references from your obstetrician and two mothers whose judgment you trust. A list of at least three possible physicians your insurance will cover should be enough.

Next, call the offices of these doctors and identify yourself as an expectant mother and a potential patient. Ask if they're accepting new patients. If they are, ask them to send or fax you their brochure or some information on their fees and newborn care. Some doctors' offices prefer a face-to-face meeting and may simply recommend that you schedule an appointment to visit the office. Either of these approaches is appropriate. This will help you determine if the front office is friendly, reliable, and capable of following up.

Whether you visit over the phone or face to face, ask yourself these questions: Did they act excited for you and your new arrival or did they treat you like just another ho-hum number? If this had been an emergency, would you have been placed on hold without first being asked why you were calling? Did they already act too busy and disinterested in taking on another patient? How long did it take for them to get you the information you requested— two days or two weeks? Did they send just the basics or did they include helpful baby brochures?

Follow up on your phone calls with a visit to their offices some afternoon around 3:00 P.M. What's the mood in the office? Are newborns seated separately from sick patients? A good pediatrics practice will put healthy infants, also known as well-baby checks, immediately into a separate room. Did the office staff recognize your presence or did you feel like they're doing you a favor by noticing you?

Ask if you can get a quick tour of the office and perhaps say hello to one of the nurses on staff. If they're not busy, but are rude or impatient with you, scratch this one from the list. Trust me, the front office and nursing staff usually convey the mood and tone of the doctor.

After you've visited the office, make an appointment with the pediatrician. Most doctors don't charge for this visit, but you should ask if they do when you schedule the appointment. This will be your ten to fifteen minutes to get acquainted with the pediatrician. If you don't find the doctor warm, friendly, excited about the baby, and willing to spend time talking with you, don't hesitate to keep looking.

Find out about specifics. Since many newborns seem to get sick after regular business hours and on weekends, ask the doctor what you should do when this happens. Who do you call and how do you reach the doctor in the evenings and on weekends? Inquire about whether or not their office has a nurse practitioner. Will you be seeing him or her when your child gets sick, or will you always be able to see the doctor? If the doctor is in a group practice, do you sense that he or she gets along with the other doctors in the practice or on-call group? Who covers for your doctor when they're not on call or while they're on vacation? Keep in mind that doctors are human beings and need vacations, time off, and sleep, just like everyone else!

Finally, ask the doctor if they're board-certified. This is the stamp of excellence for pediatricians, so you won't offend them by asking. Board certification guarantees that the doctor has passed the requirements of the American Board of Specialties covering pediatric knowledge and practice skills. New pediatricians generally can't take the boards for one or two years after their training, during which time they're called board-eligible. Older pediatricians who aren't board-certified might have completed an acceptable pediatric training program but either never took the boards or failed to pass them. If this is the case regarding one of your candidates, clarify the situation or keep looking for someone else. Remember, the most important factor in all of this is that you need a capable, intelligent pediatrician who you feel at ease with and who you have the utmost confidence in.

How Dad Picked the Pediatrician

My husband, Mark, chose our pediatrician because I was on bed rest due to a serious round of pre-term labor. Propped up on a pillow, I reviewed our insurance information to determine which pediatricians were covered. After talking with my ob-gyn and several moms for their suggestions, I made a list of my top three candidates and called to set up the interviews for Mark. Before each interview, Mark and I discussed the issues and questions we were most concerned about.

After completing two interviews, we didn't feel the need to do a third. Both doctors were well qualified and easy to interact with. After further discussion and factoring in Mark's preference, we selected our pediatrician and have been delighted with the choice ever since.

SURVIVAL TIPS FROM DR. CAROLE

I always find it so exciting to talk with prospective first-time parents. Their enthusiasm and desire to become the best parents imaginable is highly contagious. They invariably have endless questions, have read numerous guides and pamphlets, and have received lots of free advice from friends and family. So let's begin by fast-forwarding to you, the first-time parents, as you're receiving some last-minute instructions from the hospital nursery before being discharged and sent home with your new baby.

First of all, you probably haven't had a good night's sleep for at least the last month. Mom hasn't found a comfortable sleeping position since the thirty-sixth week, and every time she rolls over, the whole bed moves and Dad wakes up. Secondly, labor never seems to start early in the morning after a sound sleep! The fact is that most new parents greet the dawn with their newborn, not even realizing they're already twelve hours behind on sleep.

During the next twenty-four hours in the hospital, the whole family experiences noise, unfamiliar surroundings, and nurses checking on you every two to four hours. By now you've gone at least three nights with little or no sleep. In spite of all this, at the end of your stay, you're bid cheerful good-byes, wished good luck, and sent out the door with strict instructions to relax, enjoy, and call if you have any questions!

> Good news! Insurance companies are beginning
> to extend hospital time on healthy deliveries
> up to forty-eight hours!

As new parents, what you urgently need is basic survival parenting skills for the important things that will arise in the first few weeks at home.

You'll be amazed at how the following tips can get you through the times when you feel totally overwhelmed.

Simplify your life. The only activities you must do in the next few weeks of your infant's life is feed your baby, change your baby, and try to convince your baby that sleeping at night for long periods of time is acceptable behavior—not only acceptable, but highly desirable!

Feeding your baby. There are three basic choices for feeding your baby: breast-feed only, bottle-feed only, or both. It's okay to change your mind about your choice if it's not working well for you. Some mothers may nurse for two days, two weeks, or two years. Good moms do any or all of the above. Nursing may not be the right thing for you. This is a very individual decision and only you can decide what you would like. Don't let guilt be your deciding factor.

If you're unsure about your decision to nurse, I encourage you to try. Nothing ventured, nothing gained—right? An enthusiastic newborn with a great sucking reflex along with a supportive labor and delivery nurse can sway you to the nursing side. Remember, you can always quit and say you at least tried.

If you absolutely don't want to breast-feed, then don't. It's your body and your baby. Once again, you can be a good mom and give your baby formula.

If you decide to nurse, you should read whatever you can get your hands on about nursing before you deliver your baby. (See the appendix for some reading choices.) You must prepare your mind, Dad, and your nipples for the nursing mind-set. In fact, Dad is the number one predictor of breast-feeding success based on his support or resistance.

Baby's sleep time. I'm thoroughly convinced that trying to put your newborn on a rigid schedule immediately after birth will frustrate everyone involved. Your only goal in the first few weeks is to encourage your newborn to eat plenty during the day and sleep a great deal at night. This is much easier to accomplish with some babies than others. Each baby is a unique individual and adjusts to life outside the womb in their own way and at their own pace. With this said, getting your baby to sleep through the night by two weeks of age doesn't qualify one for Saint Motherhood either. For many babies and parents, it happens simply by the grace of God, not parental savvy!

Tips for baby's sleep time. Try not to let your baby sleep more than three hours at a time during the day. If they went to sleep at 11:00 A.M. and it's now 2:00 P.M., go wake her up! Your baby may not want to feed immediately, so this is the time to talk to her, carry her around and play with her. In other words, teach your baby to take only three-hour naps during the day. I encourage you to play, coo, and interact with your newborn as much as possible before or after daytime feedings. You don't need to walk with her every waking moment, but if possible keep her awake in an infant chair, on the floor, or in a swing.

During the day, always put your baby to sleep with some background noise, preferably a radio—anything from CNN to Mozart will do. This encourages babies to fall asleep during the day with noise, as opposed to sleeping in total peace and quiet at night. This means you don't need to tiptoe around your infant, but short of vacuuming (and if you're vacuuming during the first two weeks, you're overdoing it), do your normal noisy chores.

Try to keep your precious one awake until around 8:00 or 9:00 P.M. Then gather up all the no-nonsense in your character and repeat over and over, Nighttime is for sleeping. What this translates into is this: Baby wakes up at 11:00 P.M. Do not coo, talk, or cuddle. These are daytime activities. Change your newborn's diaper only if it's soaked or soiled, and feed her as quickly as possible with no verbal interaction. For nursing moms, this is ten minutes on one breast and fifteen to twenty minutes on the other. For bottle-fed babies, this is two ounces. Try to burp for five minutes. Continue feeding until your baby is full, or for fifteen minutes max. Then burp your precious, adorable wonder, joy of your life—change diaper again, if needed—say, *"Goodnight, Mommy/Daddy loves you,"* and put her back in the crib. Close the door firmly and note the time. She's allowed to cry vigorously for ten minutes before you go back in. If you have to go back in, check the diaper, offer a pacifier, rock or walk her—whatever, for ten minutes—but do not talk. Then go lie down again. Don't worry if it doesn't work instantly. You're trying to set a pattern and encourage sleep.

Don't rock your baby to sleep during the wee hours except as a last resort.

It's okay to let your baby cry. Babies are not permanently damaged by crying for brief periods of time, up to ten to fifteen minutes. If she's fed, warm, and dry, sometimes she just needs a good cry to settle down and sleep.

Since most homes are climate controlled during the day, your baby can sleep in a cotton or terry sleeper with a light blanket for cover. At bedtime, your baby needs additional blankets or a heavier sleeper only if you turn the heat down. It's no longer recommended that you swaddle your baby, but rather encourage free movement of hands and feet at all times. Be aware that this may be contrary to previous counsel by pediatric professionals, grandparents, nurses, or physicians.

> *It's no longer recommended that you swaddle your baby, but rather encourage free movement of hands and feet at all times. Be aware that this may be contrary to previous counsel by pediatric professionals, grandparents, nurses, or physicians.*

During the first year, you'll be working on helping your infant learn to develop good sleep habits. Some babies will be easy from the very beginning, while some will be lousy sleepers even with the best parenting techniques. It's helpful to keep track of your baby's sleep and awake times during the first several weeks to see how their sleep patterns are developing. If there's a problem, share your findings with your pediatrician during your first several visits and inquire if he or she has any hints or advice to give you.

Babies can be put in their cribs awake!

Sleep positions for baby. There have been many changes in thinking over the last several years regarding sleep positions for newborns. The American Academy of Pediatrics now recommends that all newborns be placed on their backs to sleep unless your doctor specifically instructs you otherwise. Studies have shown that babies who are put to sleep on their backs are at less risk of sudden infant death syndrome (SIDS) than those placed on their stomach to sleep.

Studies have shown that babies who are put to sleep on their backs are at less risk of sudden infant death syndrome (SIDS) than those placed on their stomach to sleep.

More on breast-feeding. Many expectant mothers spend hours agonizing over whether to breast-feed or bottle-feed. Often I find that they're inclined toward one method or the other. They simply need reassurance and encouragement. Preconceived ideas and other people's emotions can complicate one's decision. For example, some family members can be very supportive of breast-feeding, while others have a negative attitude and may even find it unnatural. Just be sure your partner supports your nursing. Ask him if he'll be comfortable with you nursing in public. Let him know that it's possible to be discreet and unobtrusive.

Breast-feeding is something only you can do for your baby. It can be viewed as a special event or it can be extremely tiring. Your partner can feel left out or he can be great at getting the baby to nuzzle to your breast. You both should realize that nursing your baby will be your number one accomplishment in the first several weeks. The emphasis will not be on preparing meals, cleaning the house, or anything else. Breast-fed babies tend to nurse more frequently during the first several weeks, so you must foresee getting up every two to three hours around the clock.

If you're considering nursing, there are some basic facts and suggestions that may shed some light on the subject:

- Breast milk or formula is all your baby needs for the first four to six months of life. Most formulas are fairly close to breast milk, except for the added antibodies that your breast milk alone can pass on to your infant. These antibodies can be important in the first several months to help your baby fight off infections. Whatever amount of breast milk your baby gets has your own antibodies, so even if you nurse only for the first week of your baby's life, she'll pick up important antibodies.

- Breast milk is convenient. It comes already prepared and is available twenty-four hours a day. However, if you plan to breast-feed exclusively, this means you'll be a twenty-four-hour convenience store.

- Formula is also convenient, but more expensive. The days of sterilizing bottles and boiling formulas are long gone. Concentrated formula merely needs to be added to warm water and put into a clean bottle.

- Breast-feeding is not an all-or-nothing decision. You can breast-feed during the day and, as a supplement, have your partner give the baby a bottle at night. If you plan to breast-feed, I strongly recommend that you breast-feed only (no bottles) during the first two weeks to get your system (body) going. Then you can supplement, quit, or keep on nursing exclusively—it's up to you.

- Not all babies will successfully nurse! Notice I said babies, not mothers. I have had several experienced mothers unable to nurse their sixth or seventh baby, even though they've had years of nursing experience and tried every trick in the world. Their babies simply did not latch on and nurse well. This is not to discourage you, but to help you realize that being able to nurse is not the ultimate test of motherhood. Babies grow up healthy and loved either on formula or breast milk.

SOME BABIES CHOOSE THE BOTTLE REGARDLESS OF A MOTHER'S EFFORTS TO BREAST-FEED.

- Read all you can about nursing. If you do decide to nurse, work on toughening up your nipples. You do this by rubbing them with a rough washcloth twice a day for two to three months prior to delivery.

- Find a close friend who has nursed successfully and ask her to be your coach. She'll have had lots of experience with things that work and don't work. Remember, though, that everyone is different, and what worked for her may not work for you.

- Don't introduce a pacifier until breast-feeding is well established. This may take up to a couple of weeks. It has been well documented that babies will nurse better if they're not given a pacifier between feedings. Your baby needs to spend time on your breast, not on the pacifier.

- Be sure you tell everyone in the nursery at the hospital that you intend to nurse your baby immediately after she's born. Make sure the nursery knows you want the baby to nurse only. Tell them specifically not to give your baby any formula! Tell them you want the baby to come to your room at night to nurse and not to give the baby a pacifier in order to let you sleep. Supplement the baby with only glucose water, sterilized water, or as recommended by your doctor until you're nursing well. Ask the nurses for help if you feel things aren't going well. It's their job and they've helped hundreds of mothers, so they should have lots of tips and suggestions.

- When you arrive home from the hospital, conserve your energy for nursing your baby. Drink lots of fluids, eat well-balanced meals, and rest whenever possible.

- If you plan to use a breast pump, don't hand express or use an inexpensive pump. Both methods tend to be inefficient and time consuming. Fast, efficient electric pumps are readily available for rent or purchase. If you're going to use a pump, why not make it easy? Pumping is a way to let your partner participate in feeding the baby by giving the baby a bottle of breast milk. It also allows you an opportunity to take a break and sleep through the night. Also, pumping is essential for women who are going back to work right away.

- If you're experiencing pain with nursing, talk to your physician. Your nipples will take a while to toughen up, but it shouldn't hurt to nurse. Pain may signify an infection, or you may simply need to position the baby differently during nursing.

- Alternate breasts so that you don't always start on the same side. Putting a safety pin on your bra works well to mark the breast you last nursed on. Each breast is different from the other. One will seem to have more milk or be fuller. This is perfectly normal. I suggest that mothers nurse for ten minutes on one breast and then nurse longer on the other breast, again starting with alternating right or left breast each feeding.

There's nothing more natural than nursing a baby. Outsiders tend to give expectant mothers all kinds of unsolicited advice. Decide what you want to do, and then find some good support people within your circle of friends, family, and health care providers.

More on bottle-feeding. I suggest you start with the formula recommended in the nursery. Do not switch formula without consulting your physician. You may receive free coupons or free formula in the mail, but again, don't substitute or buy the bargain brand without first consulting your physician.

Start with four ounces of formula at a time. Initially, feed your baby two ounces, try to burp her even if it takes several minutes, then feed your baby again until she appears full. Generally, by the end of the first month, your baby will be eating approximately four to six ounces at a feeding. Once more, every baby is different, so there are no hard-and-fast rules.

The wonderful little premixed bottles in the hospital nursery are so cute and so expensive. Powder works just as well as the premixed—you need only to follow the directions carefully. I wouldn't premix large amounts of formula ahead of time; just add warm water to the powder and shake when you're ready to feed.

Your baby will do fine on formula alone the first several months. Don't rush feeding your baby cereal. Your mother may tell you that you were eating cereal by the time you were six weeks old. Times have changed and formulas have changed. Formula alone is the best choice for your baby unless your doctor advises you otherwise.

You don't need to sterilize bottles or nipples. You can wash them in hot soapy water and rinse well or run them through the dishwasher. Use the upper rack—burning rubber is not a sweet smell!

If you don't have drinkable tap water, ask your physician what he or she recommends as suitable water. Spring water isn't safety tested and should not be used for infants.

Your baby and bowel movements. Since babies spend so much time eating, it's only natural that they spend a lot of time eliminating. Unfortunately, this means that parents spend a lot of time worrying about their infant's bowel movements. As a general rule of thumb, breast-fed babies may stool each and every time they nurse. Usually, the stool is soft (runny to mushy), yellowish in color, and has no odor. However, it's good to note that a nursing baby can sometimes go three to four days without a stool.

Bottle-fed babies generally stool every day or up to several times a day, again often after being fed. Their stools are yellow to green in color, usually formed, and can have a foul smell.

Constipation isn't often a problem in the first several weeks after birth. Most babies grunt and push with bowel movements, so unless the stool becomes pebbly and hard, this is of no concern. Again, if you have any questions, be sure to call your physician.

Your newborn from head to toe. The soft spot on your baby's head isn't as delicate as most parents fear. You can safely wash over this area without hurting your infant. Bumping their head accidentally in this area also will not harm your newborn.

Your baby can see from birth, but can't focus well. Babies see best about seven inches from an object, so this is the best distance from which to hold and talk to your infant. Babies like sharply contrasting colors; this is why many of the new toys are black and white, black and red, and so forth.

BABIES LOVE TO SUCK. THEY'LL SUCK ON FINGERS, TOES, THUMBS, OR PACIFIERS.

Infants sneeze frequently to clear their noses. This is nothing to be concerned about. In the winter, you may want to run a vaporizer to add humidity to your baby's room while she sleeps, especially if you live in a dry climate.

Be sure you understand how to take care of the umbilical cord before you leave the nursery and go home with your newborn. It takes up to two weeks for the umbilical cord to fall off. You'll need to sponge bath your baby until then. The cord may have an odor. This is normal; however, notify your doctor if there is any redness around the umbilical area or pus or bright bleeding from the umbilical cord.

Your baby's fingernails may be long immediately after delivery. Trim them (best to do while baby is sleeping) so she doesn't scratch herself.

It's not unusual for girl babies to have swollen labia due to increased hormones received from the mother during pregnancy. You'll notice a whitish drainage or discharge, which is normal. Remember to clean in and around the labia whenever bathing or changing diapers. Always wipe baby girls from front to back to prevent bacteria from spreading.

Milia are small, pinpoint white spots over the nose, cheeks, and chin which may be present during the first one to two weeks due to clogged glands. Don't squeeze them. They require no treatment and will disappear on their own. Newborn acne or zits on the baby's face may begin one to two weeks after delivery. Again, it's due to increased hormones received from the mother during pregnancy. This, too, is of no concern and will go away without treatment.

Make sure you know how to care for your infant's circumcision before you go home from the hospital. Ask how to clean and change the gauze, if needed. If you have any questions afterwards, call your doctor.

Day-to-day activities and your baby. Routines and schedules are wonderful because they bring a sense of well-being and order to our lives. It's great if your baby always takes a nap between 10:00 A.M. and noon so you can plan some part of your day. However, you want your newborn to learn to adapt to changes and new encounters. Once more, balance seems to be the key for both you and your baby. Don't be a slave to your schedule, but try to develop some guidelines and routines during the first few weeks so that you create a fair amount of consistency in your daily activities. If you have a fussy baby who is up all night, you don't need to feel guilty that your only goal during the day is to survive.

Many parents ask about when they can begin taking their babies out in public. If the weather is nice, babies can be exposed to fresh air from the day they're born. New mothers tend to overdress their newborns in warm weather. If it's eighty-five degrees outside, a light blanket is sufficient. It will also help to keep away any dirt or dust from the wind away and to shield your baby from bright sunlight.

My main concern about babies being out and about is that everyone seems to want to touch and hold a newborn, especially other children who may have colds or other infections. It's the right choice to ask people not to touch your baby. Tell them your doctor requested you keep your baby away from other people until the baby is six to eight weeks old. Mentioning doctor's orders usually solves the problem.

My main rule is that parents need to keep their new babies away from crowds, inquisitive small hands, and any sick people for a minimum of one month, preferably two months.

Grandparents can be either a huge source of encouragement and advice or a tremendous drain on energy, self-esteem, and sense of well-being. Unfortunately, there rarely seems to be a happy medium. Keep in mind that they raised you and your siblings in another era, with different medical opinions, diets, sleep patterns, and the parenting philosophies of their time. We all tend to forget that raising our own children doesn't make us experts on raising other people's children. It's your baby and your responsibility to decide what's best for your child.

If grandparents visit during the first few months, ask them to help with the cooking and housework, which will give you more time to spend with your baby. They might like to rock a fussy baby for you or give the baby a bath, but they often hesitate because times have changed so much and they feel a bit left out. Give grandmas and grandpas a chance. They do have good suggestions and you can always sort out those you want to follow. However, if they're more work than they are help, difficult as it might be, you may have to ask them to leave or come at another time.

The major fear of most new parents is that they'll do something wrong. Yes, you may do a lot of dumb things along the way that you'll laugh about later on. This is a new experience for both you and your partner, but the only way you'll learn is through patience and trial and error. Fortunately, your baby is very forgiving. If you spend ten minutes trying to figure out why she won't stop crying before you discover a dirty diaper, she'll forgive you. There's no magic set of instructions, no magic guidebook (this one is as close as you'll come), and no single set of parents have all the right answers for their baby. So relax, enjoy, and have fun on this new adventure.

TIPS FROM THE AMERICAN ACADEMY OF PEDIATRICS

The following section is an overview of the common issues many new parents face. It presents suggestions and general comments for dealing with these issues. If you have questions and concerns specific to your baby, always consult your baby's pediatrician.

JAUNDICE AND HEALTHY NEWBORNS

Jaundice is a common condition in newborn infants, showing up shortly after the baby is born. In most cases, it disappears on its own. If not, it's easily treated.

What is jaundice? A baby has jaundice when bilirubin, which is produced naturally by the body, builds up faster than a newborn's liver can break it down and get rid of it in the baby's stool. This happens for one or more of the following reasons:

- The baby's developing liver isn't yet able to remove the bilirubin from the blood

- More bilirubin is being made than the liver can handle

- Too much of the bilirubin is reabsorbed from the intestines before the baby gets rid of it in the stool

Too much bilirubin makes a jaundiced baby's skin look yellow. This yellow color will appear first on the face, then on the chest and stomach, and finally on the legs.

What is bilirubin? Everyone's blood contains hemoglobin found in red blood cells. Red blood cells live only a short time, and as they die, the oxygen-carrying substance (hemoglobin) is changed to yellow bilirubin. It's normal for newborns to have excess bilirubin because their liver isn't efficient at removing it. Older babies, children, and adults get rid of this yellow blood product quickly, usually through bowel movements.

Can jaundice hurt my baby? Jaundice can be dangerous if the bilirubin reaches too high a level in the blood. The level at which it becomes dangerous will vary based on a child's age and other medical conditions. A small sample of your baby's blood can be tested to measure the bilirubin level. Other tests may be needed to see if your baby has a medical reason for making extra bilirubin that's causing the jaundice.

How do I know if my baby has jaundice? Parents should be aware of any changes in their newborn's skin color or the coloring in the whites of their child's eyes. Look at the baby under natural daylight or in a room that has fluorescent lights. A quick and easy way to test for jaundice is to press gently with your fingertip on the end of your child's nose or forehead. If the skin looks white (this is true for babies of all races), there's no jaundice. If you see a yellowish color, contact your pediatrician and have the baby checked further for significant jaundice.

How is jaundice treated? Mild to moderate levels of jaundice don't require any treatment. If high levels of jaundice don't clear up naturally, your baby may be treated with special lights or other treatments. Some treatments require that your baby stay in the hospital for a few days. If your baby needs light therapy, talk to your pediatrician about how long the treatment lasts and where it will be done—at home or in the hospital.

Another treatment is more frequent feedings of breast milk or formula to help pass the bilirubin out in the stools. Rarely, babies may require treatment of their blood to remove the bilirubin. Your pediatrician will give you more details if other treatments are necessary.

What about jaundice and breast-feeding? Most breast-fed babies don't have a problem with jaundice that requires an interruption of breast-feeding. However, if your baby develops jaundice that lasts a week or more, your pediatrician may ask you to temporarily stop breast-feeding for a day or two. If you must temporarily stop breast-feeding, talk to your pediatrician about pumping your breasts so you can keep producing breast milk and restart nursing easily.

DIAPER RASH

Diaper rash affects most babies at some time and in varying degrees. It can result in discomfort for your baby and worry for you. However, there are things you can do to try to make your baby feel better if it does occur. By knowing what to look for, you have a much better chance of keeping your baby happy and comfortable.

What is diaper rash? Diaper rash is a term used to describe any skin irritation in the diaper area. The known causes of diaper rash include wetness, not changing diapers often enough, and a combination of urine and feces that irritates your baby's skin. Other causes include overcleansing with soaps, antibiotic usage, and yeast and germ infections. In many cases, mild diaper rash will appear with no known cause and will heal without any treatment.

How can you help prevent diaper rash? The following suggestions may help to hold off diaper rash:

- Avoid harsh soaps and don't overcleanse. Harsh scrubbing after each diaper change may damage the outer protective layer of the skin.

- Avoid using wipes with alcohol and perfumes because these products can irritate your baby's skin. Using water alone as a cleanser may be all that's necessary.

- Change diapers immediately after each bowel movement and urination. Wet skin is easily irritated by bowel movements.

- Avoid too much drying after a diaper change. Gently pat the area dry with a soft towel. You should also avoid using an electric hair dryer; this may cause windburn on your baby's sensitive skin.

- Apply a thin layer of ointment for protection against wetness and avoid perfumed lotions or powders that can irritate your baby's skin.

How can diaper rash be treated? Despite your best efforts, your baby may still get diaper rash. If this happens, there are steps you can take to help eliminate it:

- Be sure you change diapers often and avoid airtight fastening, especially overnight. You can increase air circulation within the diaper by using larger diapers and by loosely attaching them. You also can cut the elastic bands on disposable diapers for a loose fit.

- Apply a cream such as a zinc oxide paste, which stays on longer than an ointment. Desitin is one kind. It protects the baby's skin by sealing out moisture and irritants in a bowel movement.

- For major cleanups, instead of wiping your baby's skin clean, try using a running stream of warm water from a squeeze bottle. This is a gentler method for cleaning and an easy way to rinse off bowel movements and urine in the diaper area. To make the job easier, put your baby in a sink or tub for easy rinsing.

Call your pediatrician if the rash continues to worsen either on its own or during treatment. A yeast rash, a serious skin irritation, or an infection may require special medical treatment. Maintaining the pH balance of your baby's skin prevents diaper rash. Therefore, using products that maintain the pH balance are more beneficial.

Are cloth or disposable diapers better for preventing diaper rash? There are advantages and disadvantages to both cloth and disposable diapers. Because diaper rash often occurs when skin is wet and irritated, part of the diaper's job is to keep the baby dry. Cloth and disposable both work as long as they're changed often. Some children may be better suited for one type of diaper or another. Trial and error may be the best answer.

What about talcum powder? Many parents apply talcum powder to the diaper area during a change; however, routine use of talcum powder isn't recommended. If you do use it, be sure to keep it away from your infant's face, because inhaling it could cause breathing problems. Shake the talcum powder onto your hands away from the baby's eyes, nose, and mouth—and then apply it to your baby.

BABIES AND CRYING

All parents hope that their newborn will be a cuddly, cooing infant who eats well, sleeps soundly, and cries rarely. Most parents are surprised and upset to learn that the typical baby cries an average of two and one-quarter hours each day the first seven weeks of life. Your baby's crying may not bother you. However, if it does, the following information will help you understand why babies cry and better prepare you to help your baby.

Crying and normal infant development. All infants cry in the early weeks of life and for many different reasons. In the delivery room, a cry is the first breath for many infants. This first cry fully expands the lungs, which allows both the baby's heart and lungs to adapt to life outside the mother's womb.

Soon after birth, babies cry to let you know they're hungry, cold, tired, or uncomfortable. When parents respond quickly, babies soon learn to expect this response. This communication is a satisfying and important part of early parent-infant relationships.

By two or three weeks of age, most babies begin a new, different type of crying—fussy crying. This crying usually occurs about the same time every day, typically in the evening. The usual comforting methods that have worked to this point don't totally stop the crying. Thus, parents are faced with [what they think is] their first failure. Most parents compensate by trying harder to calm their baby, but this usually makes the crying worse. This is how a baby with a normal evening fussy period is labeled a colicky baby.

Normal crying patterns. Over twenty-five years ago, the noted pediatrician T. Berry Brazelton studied the crying habits of eighty normal, full-term babies from his practice for the first twelve months of their lives. The results of his study were revolutionary then and are relevant today. The eighty babies averaged two and one-quarter hours of crying a day for the first seven weeks of life. Their crying reached a peak of two and three-quarters hours a day when they were six weeks of age. Then the amount of crying decreased each week thereafter. A major portion of the crying occurred in the evening hours, between 5:00 P.M. and midnight.

The least fussy babies in the group (15 percent) cried one and one-half hours a day in the early weeks of life. The heavy fussers in the group (7.5 percent) averaged four hours daily crying from age six to eight weeks before the amount of crying began to decrease.

The fact that these well cared for, normal babies cried these amounts should convince all parents that crying isn't their fault. All babies cry for regular periods for their own reasons. Parents should do their best to meet their baby's obvious needs (food, dryness, cleanliness, etc.) and then think of the crying periods as a time for their baby to, in a sense, exercise or let off steam.

Crying typically decreases in the second six weeks of life as babies discover new ways to release tension, such as sucking their own fingers or a pacifier or watching their hands. Around twelve weeks of age, babies also begin to reach out socially to others by smiling, laughing, and interacting with everyone around her.

INFANT COLIC

At various times in the past sixty years, colic has been attributed to tensions in the home. In fact, there are many causes. The most common are maternal anxiety, inappropriate interaction between parents and baby, immaturity of the infant's gastrointestinal tract, spasms in the colon, trapped intestinal gas, allergy, a sensitivity to cow's milk protein, and faulty feeding techniques.

Today many researchers believe that one or several of these factors may be present at the same time in some infants with colic. For this reason, a diagnosis of colic is typically made only after a thorough history has been taken and a physical examination is performed in the doctor's office.

> *Babies with colic have a characteristic body language. One mother described her infant this way: "His body was doubled up when he screamed—loud, piercing screams that shattered me. He flung out his arms and legs, arched his back and angrily struggled to free himself when held. He would nurse greedily for a minute or two, then push my breast away, pull his knees up to his stomach as if in pain, and cry even more furiously. He would finally collapse, exhausted from hours of crying, only to startle himself awake ten minutes later. Then the whole routine would begin again."*

Colic affects an estimated 10 percent to 15 percent of newborns. It begins two to three weeks after birth (in premature babies, two to three weeks after the mother's due date), peaks at six weeks, and is usually over by the twelfth week or three months; hence the term three-month colic. Frequently, the crying episodes are confined to the evening hours, 6:00 P.M. to midnight. Unfortunately, this is the time when parents may be most tired and least able to cope. In a small number of infants, the crying is almost nonstop from morning to night, or the continuous crying occurs during a five- or six-hour period at some time other than during the evening.

Colic has been reported for centuries It occurs in all cultures, races, and social classes, although it may be less common in certain non-Western societies where infants are in constant physical contact with their mothers. Colic isn't related to the baby's sex, complications the mother may have experienced during pregnancy, or the type of birth. Breast-fed babies seem to be just as likely to develop colic as bottle-fed infants. And, contrary to what many believe, colic isn't more common in firstborn children. In short, there is no single common denominator among infants who develop colic.

Life after colic. Usually, when the baby is approximately twelve weeks of age, the severe crying will end. Truly it will. Sometimes it happens abruptly, almost overnight. More often than not, it's a less dramatic and more lengthy process, with the baby having fewer and fewer fussy periods. Parents may not believe that something as grim as their baby's prolonged crying will be forgotten once it's over, but this often seems to be true. The unpleasant memories fade, and a new relationship emerges. Some parents even feel that their relationship with their baby is stronger because of the crying. One mother commented, "I feel as if we've been through a tremendous struggle together—and both survived it. Now I'm determined to do all I can to help her grow and be happy."

HELPING PARENTS SURVIVE THE CRYING GAME

It's not surprising that parents of babies with colic express feelings of helplessness, rejection, guilt, frustration, resentment, and anger. A common first reaction is for the mother to blame herself; sometimes the father also blames the mother. Some women may conclude that they're not fit for motherhood and worry that their relationship with their child will be permanently damaged.

Parents need to realize that the problem is with the baby, although the baby can do nothing about it. The cause of the crying is as individual to each infant as their personality.

However, the crying arouses powerful negative emotions. A crying, inconsolable baby can reduce even the calmest, most confident parent to a distressed, helpless one. It's a normal reaction to feel intense anger toward an infant who seems so ungrateful for the parents' care and is turning life upside down.

Feelings of resentment and anger are frightening to new parents. They feel something is terribly wrong with them because they don't always feel overwhelming love for their infant. Parents must be able to admit that they have mixed feelings toward their baby. Talking about negative feelings usually lessens their power and allows positive feelings to be experienced as well.

Coping with crying. Parents whose first baby is a heavy fusser haven't had the chance to build confidence in their ability to care for an infant. If you have a baby with colic or who fusses heavily, talk the problem over with your health care practitioner. He or she might suggest a management plan to help console the baby.

Your health care practitioner will consider several factors in this plan. The temperament of the individual infant may play a role in the amount of crying he or she does. Newborns differ greatly in the degree of sensitiveness and fussiness they experience, as well as in the ease with which they can be consoled. They also differ in their sensitivity to stimulation from their own body and from the world around her.

Altering the diet for breast-feeding mothers might be suggested. Some women find that eliminating caffeine (from coffee, tea, and cola), chocolate, onions and garlic, milk and milk products, or eggs helps their baby. If the doctor suggests changes in either the baby's or the mother's diet, parents should keep in mind that this approach is trial and error. Frequent changes may not only be useless, but psychologically harmful if the return of colic leads to further frustration and depression of the parents.

Comforting techniques. Babies who fuss a lot can be divided into two groups, depending on how they respond to different soothing techniques. Babies in the first group are extremely sensitive to the surrounding world. They can't tolerate any sudden motion; even their own jerky reflexes can cause them to cry. They must be handled gently and quietly. Loud noises, bright lights, and bouncing should be avoided Feeding should take place in a quiet, darkened room away from other children.

Fussy babies in the second group thrive on bouncing and other large body movements. External stimuli such as music, motion, or body contact seem to distract these babies from their internal distress.

Parents have also found the following techniques to be effective in soothing at least some fussy babies some of the time:

- Hold your baby, keeping the infant's arms and legs close to their body with your hand, and walk or rock while talking softly.

- Carry your baby in a front carrier. The body contact and gentle motion put many fussy babies to sleep.

- Sit comfortably and hold your baby face down, with your hand under the baby's tummy. Slowly rock your legs back and forth.

- Lie on your back and put your baby face down on top of you. Gently massage the baby's back.

- Try a wind-up or battery-operated bed or swing. Be sure that the baby's head is supported.

- Take your baby out of the house for a walk. Usually, an infant's mood will change dramatically in new surroundings, especially outdoors.

To avoid overstimulating your baby, try only one or two comforting methods in each fifteen- to twenty-minute period. The longer and more intense the crying becomes, the more difficult it is to soothe the baby.

Parent support. Although the crying will eventually end, this reassuring fact doesn't always ease the difficult days and nights with a fussy baby. While parents try to ease their baby's discomfort, they also need a plan for getting themselves through the ordeal. Here are some suggestions:

- Don't take the crying personally. Fussy babies aren't mad at their parents; your baby isn't rejecting you.

- Take a break from your baby. Find a caring baby-sitter and do something for yourselves, preferably outside the home. Even an hour a day away from a colicky baby helps.

- Join a parent support group. Talk with other parents who are having the same experience. Check with local childbirth organizations about support groups for new mothers and fathers,

SUMMARY

 Newborn babies are amazingly fragile and sturdy at the same time. This unique combination can be perplexing to new parents. I hope this chapter has given you some insight into the health issues you may face during the first few months with your newborn.

 Different children have different needs in all areas of their development, whether it's sleeping, feeding, or playing. If you take away only one thing from this chapter, let it be this: When in doubt about your newborn's well-being, always call your health care professional! A pediatrician's aim is to facilitate the health and well-being of infants, and he or she wants you to call if you have questions.

DAY TRACKERS

Newborn trackers are a tool designed to help you keep a chronicle of the routine activities, like eating and sleeping, involved with caring for a newborn. Between the raging hormones and sleep deprivation, you may be amazed how easily feeding amounts and sleeping times are forgotten. If any health concerns arise, you will need to know this information when you talk with your baby's doctor. I found these little trackers a great way to bring a small bit of order to an often haphazard day during the early weeks at home with my newborn.

Newborn Daytracker

Day/Date: _____

Feeding:

Guide	Start/Side	Amount/Time	Total

Sleeping:

Guide	Start/Stop	Amount/Time

Medication: *Rx:*

Time	Item	Amount

Diaper Changes:

Wet	Soiled	Total

Notes:

Destination Family

Chapter 8

Destination Family

I believe all new parents have a strong desire to make a good home and a good life for their family. But what does that mean? Though all healthy families share some common elements, families are as unique as the people who comprise them. As parents we're called upon to care for and nurture our children in such a way that they'll grow up with the opportunity to live fully productive lives.

Stephen Covey, in his book *The 7 Habits of Highly Successful Families,* talks about the special role of parenting as a "sacred stewardship in life." He writes, "It has to do with nurturing the potential of a special human being entrusted to their [parents'] care." And he asks, "Is there really anything on any list of values that would outweigh the importance of fulfilling that stewardship well—socially, mentally, and spiritually, as well as economically?"

As with most things, the clearer the vision of what you want your family life to be, the better your chances are of achieving your goal and enjoying the subsequent benefits. Hence, my objective in this chapter is to help you identify and define what family life means to you. By showing you some of the pitfalls and payoffs of parenthood and offering you some tools for exploration, I hope you'll be inspired to pursue a deeper study of your own family values and commitment to parenting.

GREAT EXPECTATIONS

Most parents will tell you that living as a family with children takes a special kind of balancing act. Both Mom and Dad will find that flexibility and adaptability are essential survival skills. As I said before, it's a big mistake to think that things won't change or that the baby will just have to fit into our world. Becoming parents really doesn't work that way. However, it's equally a mistake for parents to sacrifice their own needs and desires while trying to become the mythical perfect parent. Healthy families are those who value and respect the needs of each individual member.

Regardless of whether you've carefully planned and waited for the right time to have a child, or pregnancy has come as a grand surprise, deep inside you already have hopes, dreams, and great expectations about what it will be like to have a newborn in your life. The big question is: Do you and your partner have similar expectations? The even bigger question is: Are you willing to make the adjustments in your everyday routines, relationships, and ways of communicating to realize your desired family lifestyle?

With many couples, one or both of the partners may believe that a new baby will bring them closer together and give them a deeper sense of "us." Although in time this may be true, initially newborns tend to have the opposite effect—they often push couples apart, revealing hidden or unrecognized differences in their relationship. Often, adult partners can agree to disagree about any given issue, but when a child becomes involved, this becomes no longer acceptable to one or both individuals.

Stephen Covey provides great insight when he writes, "If you carefully consider the problems people face in marriage, you'll find that in almost every case they arise out of conflicting role expectations and are exacerbated by conflicting problem-solving strategies. . . . Conflicting [personal] scripts most often reveal themselves in two closely related areas, and the gift of self-awareness is the key to understanding both. The first is in the area of values and goals—or the way things should be—and the second is in the area of assumptions about the way things are."

Physiology and socialization cause men and women to feel, think, and perceive the world in dramatically different ways. Few things will highlight this more than the birth of a baby. As a couple, your fundamental values and philosophies may be essentially compatible. However, once you become parents, you may be shocked to find that you have different ideas about how to conduct the activities of daily life.

These differences are probably present in a marriage pre-baby, but the coping mechanisms used to manage these differences before the baby is born are disrupted or canceled out when a baby comes. Now when differences about values and ethics arise, couples are forced to deal with them if they hope to have harmony in the guidance of their child.

Take a look at your and your partner's childhoods. You may see some differences that could be potential hazards. There's a strong tendency for parents to repeat the patterns they've experienced growing up, regardless of whether or not they agree with the methods that were used. Because it's common to repeat the past, we must be aware of our desires to change and be persistent about making those changes.

The Penn State Child and Family Development Project, in its book *The Transition to Parenthood*, takes a look at the changes in a marriage after the arrival of a child. With few exceptions, couples approach parenthood with high hopes and soaring dreams. However, instead of experiencing a new and deeper closeness, after only a few months they find themselves baffled by the discovery that they have some diametrically opposed viewpoints and a marriage that's in a tailspin. The data from the Penn State project suggests that there are six important characteristics needed to facilitate a couple's smooth passage through this transition to parenthood. They are the ability to:

1. Surrender individual goals and needs and work together as a team.

2. Resolve differences about division of labor and work in a satisfactory manner.

3. Handle stress in a way that doesn't overstress a partner or a marriage.

4. Fight constructively and maintain a pool of common interests despite different priorities.

5. Realize that however good a marriage becomes post-baby, it will not be good in the same way it was pre-baby.

6. Maintain the ability to communicate in a way that continues to nurture the marriage.

In brief, if you have these abilities, you'll most likely see your marriage grow stronger, richer, and warmer—everything you hoped your marriage and family would be. Conversely, if you don't already have or develop these attributes, you may find that parenthood and your relationship with your spouse are not all you had hoped for. The good news is that individuals can acquire and improve the tools that will help them arrive at their desired destination: a great life together as a family.

STRENGTHENING THE TEAM

Since we live in a time that puts a great deal of emphasis on individuality and individual pursuits, most of us could use some sharpening of our team skills. The notion that it takes a village to raise a child certainly has merit. Unfortunately, many of us don't have an extended family nearby to provide support, assistance, and the wisdom of experience.

We may live far away from our families, in places very different from where we grew up. It's easy to spend most of our time working, driving in our cars, and talking on the phone, relatively isolated from the kind of social contact typical of the close-knit neighborhoods of years gone by. Therefore, I believe it becomes even more critical that we choose to work intimately with our partners to forge an interdependent partnership, not just roommates sharing a dwelling.

To be successful parents and enjoy a healthy family, the ability to work together as a team is essential. Achieving this goal requires that on occasion we make trade-offs in order to achieve what's best for the family as a whole. Accordingly, we must continually strive to balance our individual satisfaction and group fulfillment with a harmonious combination. Some days it works better than others!

Real-Life Trade-offs

My husband and I were married for seven years before we had our first child. As I said earlier, we were the classic DINK couple (dual income, no kids). In retrospect, it seems that in many ways we were individuals running on parallel tracks. We worked long hours, traveled independently as needed for our respective businesses, and rendezvoused for dinners and weekends. Granted, this is an oversimplification. Yet, I wouldn't have described our life together as team oriented.

Things have changed a lot since those early days. Now we're the classic OINK couple (one income, and nothing but kids.) After fifteen years of marriage and eight-plus years of parenting, we're just beginning to understand the full meaning of what it means to live as a team—financially, recreationally, and as parents. To be effective, both partners have to know what the rules are, what positions they each play, and they must absolutely be able to depend on each other to hold up their end of the bargain. My husband and I are finally getting the rules clarified and written down on paper—together!

Partnership Roles

The shift in notions about spousal roles in recent years has resulted in an infinite variety of approaches and routines. Certainly for our grandparents and many of our parents, their responsibilities were self-evident. In today's world of dual incomes and distinctly different lifestyles, such clarity is no longer obvious. An advantage for today's couples is that they're much freer to design their own unique ways of parenting. In theory, this sounds great; in application, it requires a great deal of thoughtful planning and ongoing communication.

With this new freedom, couples have the additional task of negotiating each partner's role and subsequent responsibilities within their family. This requires identifying and clarifying your expectations—a process that's best begun well before your little bundle of joy arrives on the scene.

This is especially true if you're a two-career family. When both partners have been working full time outside the home, the change to having one partner stay home with the baby full time is dramatic. Each partner's ideas about what it means to work in the home and outside the home may turn out to be substantially different. I strongly recommend that you discuss both roles and talk about how each of you would feel about being home part time or full time. Maybe Dad would prefer to spend more time at home. The possible combinations are infinite. As you begin to assess how you and your partner will collaborate in caring for your child, here are some things to consider:

- What does each of you currently contribute to the family finances?

- How much of each of your incomes goes toward paying monthly living expenses?

- How are the domestic responsibilities currently divided? Will this be appropriate once the baby arrives?

- How will each of you find time for rest and recreation? Are you willing to help your partner with this?

- How do you manage nighttime feedings if both of you are working?

- Will both of you participate in all aspects of the care and feeding of your infant when the baby arrives home?

- What aspects of caring for a newborn are you most comfortable with and concerned about (for example, feeding, bathing, clipping nails, or umbilical cord care)?

Addressing these issues before your baby comes will be invaluable and may prevent the hurt feelings or the harsh words that can happen during the course of adjusting to the new responsibilities of your parenting lifestyle.

If you haven't already done so, I urge you to begin negotiating your team strategies, the rules of the participation, and a "playbook" before your baby arrives on the sidelines. Most likely, there will be endless additions and re-negotiations as the years go by, but getting the basics down early can only help you get off to a great start.

RELATIONSHIPS OLD AND NEW

Inevitably, there will be some shuffling and redefining of your existing relationships once you begin having children. It's a natural part of the process. Life has many chapters, and our friends and family may play different roles in each. The dynamics of your relationship with your family of origin, your in-laws, and, most importantly, your partner will change—and that isn't necessarily a bad thing!

You'll have the chance to manage these changes in ways that open new channels of communication and bring about deeper levels of intimacy and appreciation. I'm convinced that open and honest communication, focused on the win/win elements of each relationship, is the key to maintaining lasting friendships.

Don't discard friends or social ties simply because they don't have young children. Trust me, there will be times when you'll be delighted to talk about anything but kids. This is especially true as your children grow older. Having balance in your life means having a well-rounded group of friends and acquaintances of all ages and from all walks of life.

Becoming a parent tends to influence the way you're viewed by your family, friends, and the rest of society. You're now held to a new level of accountability, regardless of your age or other obligations. For example, if you're a young working mother, your boss may or may not be understanding of your new responsibilities as a parent with regard to time-off, overtime, and business dinners.

For better or worse, the way you care for your child and adjust to being a parent influences how others judge you as an individual. Your interaction with family, friends, and coworkers is often evaluated in light of your conduct as a parent. For better or worse, everyone seems to have an opinion about how parents should do things. Such evaluations may consist of anything from what you feed or don't feed your child, to how you dress your child (especially in relation to the current weather conditions) or how often you use a baby-sitter. My advice is, Don't take any comments too seriously. When in fact you do need advice, ask for it. Otherwise, you can let most of the shoulds you hear go in one ear and out the other.

One of the biggest changes in your social life, particularly for the primary caregiver, is that all activities are planned around the care of your infant. Things to ask yourself:

- Can the baby be included? Do you need to arrange for a sitter?

- Do you cancel plans if the baby becomes ill?

- When will the baby need to eat and sleep?

All of your daily obligations, plus the fun things like taking walks, playing tennis, going to the gym, meeting someone for lunch, and even making telephone calls, become a new challenge.

If you work outside the home and are also the primary caregiver, it becomes even more challenging to make all the pieces fit. But with time it will come together.

The first step to mastering the art of life with baby, while at the same time keeping up some semblance of a social life, is to think about who you most enjoy spending your time with and where you most like to spend it. If you love to take walks, go out for cappuccino, or would like to be in a book club, choose to spend your social time with the people who share your interests and love you and your baby.

In the beginning, it may often be more convenient for others to come to you. Invite a close friend over for a brown bag lunch or afternoon tea. As your baby grows older, typically you'll delight in opportunities to get out of the house to go elsewhere, and so will your baby!

> *Starbucks is a popular new mommy hangout,*
> *at least in my area!*

It's important to consider which friends and family members support the changes a baby brings to your world. These are probably the relationships you'll want to invest the most time and energy in. Friends without children who don't share an interest in baby things may not fit into your schedule for a time—maybe in the future, but probably not until your child enters school full time or you hire a full-time nanny. It's better if you surround yourself with people who are supportive, flexible, and can accommodate your unpredictable schedule.

If you have time before your baby arrives, rent the classic movie The Joy Luck Club *and watch it with your mom. I did. If it does for you and your mother what it did for us, you'll be opening up whole new channels of communication and wonderful ways of looking at each other.*

DESIGNING YOUR PARENTING PHILOSOPHY

Parenting isn't a cloning process, nor is it an opportunity to relive your life through your child! It's one of life's miracles to see you and your partner's features in this incredible newborn baby. My daughter's eyes are shaped like mine, yet her eyebrows move independently like her father's. The tops of her ears are shaped like mine, the bottom halves are shaped like her father's, and so on and so forth. Much of her behavior and attitude reflect the two of us as well—an amazing blend of us into a new, unique person.

Although there are identifiable features and behaviors that all kids take from their parents, each child is a unique being. Based on that premise, a primary tenet of my parenting philosophy is to respect each child as an individual and as a person. From the very beginning, I've endeavored to nourish my daughter's ability to express her preferences and make her own choices whenever appropriate.

As time goes by, my parenting methods adjust from one developmental phase to the next, but my goal remains the same— to be a family of mutual respect and devotion. I'm committed to nurturing my children in such a way that they thrive, and not merely survive as a means for my vicarious fulfillment.

Now it's your turn! As you begin to choose your personal philosophy and methods of parenting, consider the source of any theory or practice you come across and decide to borrow. Who is the source? It could be an author, family member, or friend. What generation is the information or advice coming from? Do you share the same view of life as the advice-giver? Always ask yourself these kinds of questions before you accept, reject, or adopt a practice for raising your child.

The following tidbits are food for thought that I've come across during my parenting pilgrimage. I expect this list to grow and change with time and experience.

Each member of the family counts! Living as individuals in a family unit requires all members to take turns having things their way. No one should be expected to constantly have their own way or deny their needs in favor of the others. A healthy family calls for a reasonable balance of trade-offs between individual needs and what's best overall for the entire family.

There's no way to show your baby too much love and affection. An abundance of love and affection is essential to the well-being and healthy development of a baby. As the months go by and babies become more mobile, setting boundaries and providing guidance along with love and affirmation is a winning combination.

Don't get caught up in the baby comparison game. When you spend time with other mothers and young babies, avoid the temptation to compare your baby with others in a competitive way. Although there are developmental phases that all babies go through, each individual child blossoms and grows in their own way and time. Taking a competitive attitude about your baby's development only depletes your personal joy and diminishes the emotional closeness you can share with other new mothers.

Flexible routines and boundaries help babies feel safe and secure. Most babies thrive when they have a routine for eating and sleeping. Feeding and napping schedules should be flexible enough to meet the particular needs that arise each day, yet these timetables should also provide a framework around which you can organize daily tasks and events.

Don't be afraid to change your mind and methods if something's not working. Sometimes you need to take the trial-and-error approach to raising a child. It's great to read books and find out how others care for their babies, but in the end, you have to develop your own system, one that works for you and your child. If a feeding or sleeping method isn't working after trying it for a reasonable amount of time, try something new—and keep trying other approaches until you've found a solution.

Lead by example more than by your words. Although this practice becomes more relevant as your child gets older, it's never too early to start. Children are like little sponges, absorbing everything around them. Verbal direction is a small part of what they take in. Other people's behavior constitutes a much larger message and influence. Set an example of the kind of person you'd like your child to become. If there's something in your life you've been wanting to change, or if you're currently behaving in a way you wouldn't want your child to behave, now is the time to change it!

Keep learning and growing as a parent and a person. One of the best things you can do for yourself, your partner, and your child is to be committed to a lifestyle that values continued growth. Whether it's a career (homemaking is a career), hobby, community service, or a combination of endeavors, pursuing your interests with passion makes you a more interesting human being. There is no better thing to pass on to your children than a passion for living.

FAMILY MISSION STATEMENT

When setting out on an expedition, what self-respecting explorer goes without a map, a plan, and an intended destination? As a new parent responsible for guiding a young life, it's a good idea to have a plan for where you'd like to take your family. Ideally, you and your partner would have a mutually agreed-upon objective in mind. Often, though, this isn't the case.

It's amazing how many people choose to let circumstance and fate direct their path, taking a wait-and-see approach to life. The problem with this is that it puts them in a reactive mode rather than a proactive mode. One way to take a proactive posture is to design a family mission statement.

A family mission statement creates a tangible representation of your hopes, dreams, and desires for your family. It also serves as a compass to guide your choices in all areas of life and provides the framework that directs the plans and activities of a family's daily routine, so that life has meaning and individual lives are fulfilled.

For example: You're asked to serve on a new committee for a local charity. It's a fine organization, but it'll require one evening per month to attend the board meetings and additional time to prepare for and participate in two annual events. Ask yourself: How does this fit in with my other time commitments? How will this impact my family time? Does this satisfy my objectives in community service?

Your family mission statement should contain the priorities and parameters needed to make such decisions. It might be helpful for both parents to make personal mission statements first and then work together to build a family mission statement, incorporating the appropriate material from the personal statements.

In *The 7 Habits of Highly Effective Families*, Stephen Covey says, "It's deciding what kind of family you really want to be and identifying the principles that will help you get there. And that decision will give context to every other decision you make. It will become your destination. It will act like a huge, powerful magnet that draws you toward it and helps you stay on track."

Probably you won't have all this in place before your baby arrives. However, every bit of thought and conversation you and your partner invest in designing your own family mission statement will be rewarded many times over. If you're excited about this concept and motivated to put it into practice, read Covey's book as well as some of the other excellent resources listed in the appendix.

COMMUNICATION IS THE KEY

Relationships are an intricate mixture of love and commitment, common values and interests, and a bit of luck. An intimate relationship can be one of the most joyful but also the most profoundly painful experiences in life. The connection between two people is complicated to begin with; adding a new member to your family increases the complexity exponentially and will change the nature of your relationship in ways that are impossible to predict. So why not stack the odds in your favor?

One of the essential elements in managing and maintaining healthy relationships is effective communication. When do you feel most understood and close to your partner? Where, when, and how do you discuss important issues, ideas, and feelings? What are the areas or issues that cause friction or hurt feelings between you and your partner?

By implementing and strengthening the skills that characterize successful couples, it's possible to avoid many of the pitfalls of the misunderstandings and conflicting expectations that arise with parenting. To do this you should honestly examine how you communicate with your partner and the strengths and weaknesses of your relationship. Continue to strengthen the behaviors that are working and revise or eliminate those that are detrimental to you, your partner, and the relationship.

The essential skills for successful relationships include: listening, the ability to communicate clearly, the art of negotiation, the capacity to handle anger appropriately, and problem-solving proficiency. The following is a checklist of points for evaluating and improving your own communication with your partner:

Honesty with Diplomacy

Be honest with yourself first! Then be honest with your partner. Here's where diplomacy becomes key. What do you think, feel, and want from your relationship? What do you want for your baby and your family? Once you've answered these questions, present them in a style, time, and place that will allow your partner to receive them in a favorable light. (Please understand that I'm advocating common sense and finesse, not manipulation or deception.) The point is to be aware of the way you present your message. Using a harsh or defensive tone can diminish the content of your message and spoil the outcome of your interaction. In such a case, your partner will most likely respond to your tone rather than the information you're presenting.

> You and your partner have planned a date for a quiet dinner and maybe a movie for this Saturday night at 5:30 P.M. When Saturday arrives, your partner decides to play golf with a friend. He shows up at home at 6:00 P.M., hot, sweaty, and tired. He'd forgotten about your date together. What do you do now? Get angry, really let him have it? Would you pout, give him the silent treatment and skip the date? Ask him how his golf game was and if he'd still like to go out on a date? Or you could do something more rational like let him know how much you've been looking forward to spending some time alone with him and you'd like to go out as soon as he can shower and change. I know it's more fun to get mad, but tossing in a little maturity brings amazing results!

Given the preceding scenario, you have several choices on how to proceed. Depending on whether this late arrival is a habitual thing or rarely happens, your approach may differ. One crucial thing to consider, in either case, is that anger is a secondary emotion that occurs as a result of disappointment, hurt feelings, or broken expectations. If you can get in touch with your initial feeling about this situation and approach your conversation from that point rather than anger, you're likely to reach a far better outcome.

When, Where and How

Always avoid discussing important or potentially controversial issues when you're tired and hungry, out of sorts, or in a setting that doesn't provide any privacy. If you do, chances are good that you won't reach your objective. Ask your partner to postpone the discussion until the conditions improve. If that's not possible, take a deep breath, relax, and try to clear your mind of other distractions. If you can focus on your objective, you'll have a better chance of reaching a mutually satisfying outcome.

A Difference of Perspective:

On a weekly, if not daily, basis, I'm reminded that it's rare for any two people to view an event in the same way. We all see the world through our own unique perspective. This perspective is based on our past experiences, beliefs, and opinions. Using this definition of perspective, it's easy to see why two partners may have widely varying viewpoints on any given issue or event involved with parenting

It's helpful to have some exploratory discussions about the roles and expectations each of you has about parenting and caring for a newborn infant. An example that most parents face almost immediately is how they will respond to their infant's crying. How do you think you'll respond and why? Generally, partners have different responses and tolerances for a crying baby.

Note: Without making a conscious choice to do otherwise, we often repeat what we heard and experienced in our own families of origin, whether or not we agree with the behavior. We recommend making proactive choices about how you'll parent, rather than using reflex responses.

What Did You Expect?

Tightly entwined with perspective and attitudes are expectations. Our expectations are based on our values, beliefs, assumptions, and probably most significant, our past experiences. Our assumptions about how people should act are translated into rules that we suppose our partners share and will obey. When a rule is broken, conflict arises.

An easy example to start with is the decision about who changes diapers—Mom, Dad, or both? To continue this process, you may want to review household chores, child care tasks like feeding and bathing, and how both partners will make time to meet their own personal needs. Identifying your expectations and the ensuing rules for acceptable behavior now will give you and your partner an opportunity to discuss and negotiate such matters in an emotionally neutral setting, before an actual conflict arises (not to mention raging hormones and sleep deprivation).

If you're interested in pursuing this area in more depth, there are many excellent resources available in the appendix.

REKINDLING THE ROMANCE

After bearing two children and spending five and one-half years muddling through it all, I believe I've come across some of the key issues for jump-starting the romance with your partner after your little one arrives. Of course, I've had to experience a few land mines along the way, but I've carefully noted helpful comments and insightful advice, from which I've sorted out the best to share with you.

> *To all new mothers: If your partner doesn't read any other part of this book, do yourself a favor and make sure he reads this section. You could photocopy it and put it in his lunch bag or briefcase.*

So what is romance anyway? Most likely it has its own special elements for each individual. At a recent class on romance and relationships, I was intrigued to hear that imagination is an inherent part of romance. As I thought about it, it began to make sense to me. If you think back to when you first met your partner, I'd be willing to bet that you spent more than a few moments thinking about what your future relationship would be like. This probably included some fantasizing about candlelit evenings, weekends away, and eventually, what it would be like spending your lives together. All of these mental activities require imagination.

Do you and your partner have a favorite song, maybe one that reminds you of a special event or place? If you hear it on the radio, does it stir up old memories and entice you to make some new ones? During courtship, it's normal to spend significant time and energy planning dates, buying gifts and cards "just because," and counting the moments until you see your beloved again. Maybe you envision spending evenings together snuggling on the sofa in front of the fire or watching a movie. One of my personal favorites is when I see my husband coming through the door at a restaurant or through the crowd at an airport to meet me. A scene like this is usually followed by a big hug and a great kiss.

It's clear from these examples that being in love isn't only an emotional state, it's a condition that involves action. When we're newly in love, we behave in ways that attract, encourage, and magnify the best things about being together. In time, little by little, the mundane routines and realities of life push out these activities that ignite and sustain the romance in our relationship.

Another thing that seems to happen as a relationship matures is that we begin to sit back and wait for our partner to initiate the romance. Suddenly, we've gone from effortlessly showering our partner with endless expressions of love to a miserly "What has he/she done for me lately" attitude, which often results from feeling unappreciated. The additional responsibilities and changes in routine that come with pregnancy and new babies can quickly exaggerate and intensify these feelings.

The solution: Don't wait another minute before you reignite your imagination. Here's a little suggestion if you need some help getting started. At your first opportunity, implement the ten-second kiss! Count to ten or watch the second hand on a clock for ten seconds. How often to you kiss your partner for ten seconds or more when leaving or greeting each other? (If you're already doing this, pat yourself on the back and send me your ideas on romance for the next edition of this book!) You'll be amazed what this can do. It's a bit like pushing the first domino—who knows where it'll take you. If Mom is the one to initiate this, it'll be the best surprise Dad has had maybe since you told him you were pregnant. (Just be careful not to give him a heart attack!) An important side note: Moms, be open to receive your partner's affection, and Dads be gentle and gradual in the giving of your affection.

Not surprisingly, with a few rare exceptions sex becomes an intensely delicate subject for most couples after delivery. This shouldn't be hard to understand, considering the amount of trauma a woman's body experiences while delivering a six- to ten-pound baby. Fortunately, as with most things, time heals, and the memories of the less desirable details of pregnancy and delivery fade quickly. Let's face it, how many families would have more than one child if this weren't the case?

So men, take heart! Your sex life will probably improve significantly as time goes by. How much time? A lot of that depends on you. The biggest mistake you can make is to pressure your partner into having sex again before she's ready. You may have to endure a few more weeks or months of abstinence and limited sexual connection before you're able to return to normal relations. But this is a small price to pay for your beautiful new baby and the lasting affection of the woman you love.

Physical healing from either a vaginal or Cesarean delivery requires a minimum recovery time of four to six weeks before intercourse is medically advisable. In the cases of many new mothers, sex doesn't rank as a priority often for as long as three to six months. When we consider their hormones and sleep deprivation, it's not so hard to understand. Now Dad is probably wondering how he can help improve the odds that he'll get lucky sooner rather than later, once the physical recovery is complete, right? Well, I've got some ideas that'll make you both happy!

SEVEN WAYS TO BECOME IRRESISTIBLE TO A NEW MOM!

To be sure, the birth of a child changes a father's world, too. But unless Dad is the baby's primary caregiver, the impact on his day-to-day life is significantly less. So here are some ideas for Dad to help get his post-baby relationship off to a great start:

1. Take care of all your own stuff. With all the new baby paraphernalia around, the last thing a mom needs is someone else to clean up after. Hang up your clothes, put away the dishes, throw away the newspapers without being asked, and you'll be adding up big bonus points.

2. Help out with the laundry and other household chores. If you don't do this already, then now is a great time to start. I'm sure Mom will be happy to point you in the right direction, and then you can take the initiative yourself. Vacuuming is a big help and a simple thing to do. Also, stacking dishes or rinsing them off and putting them in the dishwasher will be sincerely appreciated.

3. Prepare dinner twice a week. This means from start to finish—buy it, prepare it, serve it, clean it up. If you don't know how to cook, no problem. Get a takeout pizza or stop by the deli in your grocery store on your way home from work. Frankly, a peanut butter sandwich with an apple and a glass of milk would

probably do fine, as long as Mom doesn't have to make it herself. If you just happen to be a gourmet chef, then Mom is the one who got lucky!

4. The surprise bubble bath. This is a surefire winner! While Mom is giving the baby her bedtime feeding, run a nice warm bath, light a few candles, and turn on some soft, relaxing music. If you start this early on, by the time she's physically healed, who knows, perhaps she'll be the one initiating your first romantic encounter post-baby.

5. Rent Mom's favorite video. Now that she's been fed and bathed, and before the next baby feeding, pop in a movie. I recommend you stay with the lighter fare—a romantic comedy, a light classic, or her favorite escape from reality selection.

6. Take the baby on an outing. Since you arrived home from the hospital with your new baby, chances are Mom hasn't been alone in the house. Having an hour or two to relax, catch up on correspondence, read, or take a nap is a real treat for her during this time. So put the baby in a stroller and go for a walk, or take the baby with you to a friend's or family member's house. You may be surprised how much fun you'll have together, just you and the baby.

7. Help Mom get the rest and nourishment she needs. Let her know every day how much you appreciate what she's accomplished and remind her to pay attention to her own needs. Help facilitate whatever needs to be done. If her needs aren't met, sooner or later the whole family will suffer.

SUMMARY

 Remembering how fragile a woman's feelings are during the first few months of being a mom may help you to understand that one of the best ways to speed up your partner's recovery is to be an encouragement and support to the woman you love. Nothing that I know of makes a woman feel more affectionate toward her partner than being treated with appreciation and admiration. In the same way, lack of appreciation and esteem, combined with stress and hurt feelings, will extinguish any sparks of romance.

 New dads have their own ways of adapting and recuperating from the birth experience, and in most cases, they differ from mom's. So be honest—ever so gently—about your needs and wishes and share them with your partner. Just remember to do so before things build up and squash your diplomacy. The entire family will benefit from your tender touch and kind-hearted approach.

To all new dads. We hereby recognize and appreciate all your efforts and participation throughout the birthing process. Clearly, we couldn't have done it without you. **Well done!**

Closing Comments

Chapter 9

Closing Comments

We've covered a lot of territory together, and I congratulate you for investing the time and energy to prepare for your imminent role as a parent! I hope I've provided you with many useful tools and ideas to help you through the transition to parenthood. More importantly, I hope I've stimulated some worthwhile thoughts and meaningful conversations between you and your partner.

Healthy families don't just happen! They emerge through devoted care, built on a foundation of love, trust, and mutual admiration—no small feat, especially today. Though it seems that the stress on today's families has reached a new high, I imagine that parents of every generation have found the task of raising a family a daunting one in the conditions of their own time.

As a parent, I urge you to inscribe the hopes and dreams that you have for your child deeply in your heart. Hold tight to all your enthusiasm and desire to be a good parent—it will serve you through the good times and the bad. Life as a family is both an awesome and an arduous journey, one of truly divine plan, filled with incomparable abundance and well worth the trek.

My hope for all new parents is that they'll look beyond the daily responsibilities and mundane chores to enjoy the wonder of the little person blossoming before their eyes. It's so easy to "not see the forest for the trees," especially during the first few months. How sad it would be to miss the magical moments of this time by getting caught up in the pandemonium of change. A wise soul reminded me on a particularly difficult day that "the laundry will always be there tomorrow, a magic moment may not, so enjoy your child today!"

Appendix

RESOURCES

Some of the resources listed below will be very helpful to you on a day-to-day basis. Others are crisis intervention resources that I hope you'll never have to use, but I thought they should be included.

National Support and Information

Child Help USA	800-422-4453
Doulas of North America	www.dona.com
National Adoption Center	800-862-3678
National AIDS Hotline	800-342-2437
Spanish	800-344-7432
National Alcohol & Drug Abuse Hotline	800-252-6465
National Center for Missing	
& Exploited Children	800-843-5678
Poison Control	800-876-4766
Postpartum Support,	
International	805-967-7636
E-mail: jhonikman@earthlink.net	

Regional and Local Organizations
(Check your local listings)

American Heart Association
Family Service Agency
La Leche League (Breast-feeding support groups)
MOPS (Moms of Pre-schoolers)
Postpartum Education for Parents (PEP)
Regional Poison Control
Shelter Services for Women and Children

Website
BabyCenter.com—An extensive website of articles and resources on topics ranging from newborn development to postpartum mothercare.

Magazines
American Baby
Child
Christian Parenting Today
Parenting
Parents
Working Mother

Catalogs

Back to Basics Toys	800-356-5360
Land's End Kids' Catalog	800-734-5437; www.landsend.com
Lilly's Kids	800-285-5555; www.lillianvernon.com
One Step Ahead	800-274-8440; www.onestepahead.com
Perfectly Safe	800-837-5437; www.kidsstuff.com
Pottery Barn Kids	800-430-7373; www.potterybarnkids.com
The Right Start	800-548-8531; www.rightstart.com
The Safety Zone	800-999-3030; www.safetyzonecatalog.com
Storybook Heirlooms	800-688-1573; www.storybookheirlooms.com

BIBLIOGRAPHY

Bingham, Mindy, and Sandy Stryker. *Things Will Be Different for My Daughter.* New York: Penguin Group, 1995.

Brazelton, T. Berry, M.D. *On Becoming a Family.* New York: Delacort Press, 1981.

_____. *Infants and Mothers: Differences in Development.* New York: Delacort Press, 1983.

_____. *What Every Baby Knows.* New York: Delacort Press, 1988.

_____. *Toddlers and Parents: A Declaration of Independence.* New York: Delacort Press, 1989.

Carson, Dr. Lillian. *The Essential Grandparent: A Guide to Making a Difference.* Deerfield Beach, Fla.: Health Communications, Inc., 1996.

Clayman, Charles B., ed. *The American Medical Association's Family Medical Guide.* 3d ed. New York: Random House, 1994.

Cooke, Courtney. *The Best Baby Shower Book.* Minnetonka, Minn.: Meadowbrook Press, 1986.

Covey, Stephen R. *The 7 Habits of Highly Effective Families.* New York: Golden Books, 1997.

Curtis, Glade B., M.D. *Your Pregnancy: Every Woman's Guide.* Tucson: Fisher Books, LLC, 1999.

Eisenberg, Arlene, et al. *What to Expect When You're Expecting.* New York: Workman Publishing Co., 1991.

_____. *What to Eat When You're Expecting.* New York: Workman Publishing Co., 1986.

_____. *What to Expect the First Year.* New York: Workman Publishing Co., 1989.

_____. *What to Expect from the Toddler Years.* New York: Workman Publishing Co., 1989.

Elium, Jeanne, and Don Elium. *Raising a Family: Living on Planet Parenthood.* Berkeley, Calif.: Celestial Arts Publishing, 1997.

Frisch, Melvin J., M.D., and Gayle Rapoport. *Getting Pregnant!* Los Angeles: The Body Press, 1987.

Griffith, H. Winter, M.D. *Complete Guide to Pediatric Symptoms, Illness and Medications.* Los Angeles: The Body Press, 1989.

Huggins, K. *The Nursing Mother's Companion.* Boston: Harvard Press, 1991.

Keith, D., et al., eds. *Breastfeeding Twins, Triplets and Quadruplets: 195 Practical Hints for Success.* Chicago: The Center for Study of Multiple Birth, 1982.

Kenison, Katrina, and Kathleen Hirsch, eds. *Mothers.* New York: North Point Press, 1996.

La Leche League International. *The Womanly Art of Breast Feeding.* Franklin Park, Ill., 1987.

Lansky, Bruce. *The Very Best Baby Name Book in the Whole Wide World.* Minnetonka, Minn.: Meadowbrook Press, 1996.

Lansky, Bruce, and Barry Sinrod. *The Baby Name Survey Book.* Minnetonka, Minn.: Meadowbrook Press, 1998.

Leach, Penelope. *Your Baby and Child: From Birth to Age Five.* New York: Alfred A. Knopf, 1980.

Lipper, Ari, and Joanna Lipper. *Baby Stuff: A No-Nonsense Shopping Guide for Every Parent's Style.* New York: Dell Publishing, 1997.

McKay, Matthew, Ph.D., et al. *Couple Skills: Making Your Relationship Work.* Oakland, Calif.: New Harbinger Publications, Inc., 1994.

Miller, Sherod, Ph.D., et al. *Straight Talk: A New Way to Get Closer to Others by Saying What You Really Mean.* New York: Rawson, Wade Publishers, Inc., 1981.

Price, A., and N. Bamford. *The Breastfeeding Guide for the Working Woman.* New York: Simon & Schuster, Inc., 1983.

Reiser, Paul. *Babyhood.* New York: Rob Weisbach Books, 1997.

Samalin, Nancy, and Catherine Whitney. *Love and Anger: The Parental Dilemma.* New York: Penguin Books, 1991.

_____. *Loving Each One Best: A Caring and Practical Approach to Raising Siblings.* New York: Bantam Books, 1996.

Schultz, Ron, and Sam Schultz. *How to Pamper Your Pregnant Wife.* Minnetonka, Minn.: Meadowbrook Press, 1997.

Simkin, P., et al. *Pregnancy, Childbirth, and the Newborn.* Minnetonka, Minn.: Meadowbrook Press, 1991.

Swinney, Bridget, M.S., R.D. *Eating Expectantly.* Minnetonka, Minn.: Meadowbrook Press, 1991.

Steede, Kevin, Ph.D. *10 Most Common Mistakes Good Parents Make and How to Avoid Them.* Rocklin, Calif.: Prima Publishing, 1998.

Wagner, Hilory. *The New Parents Source Book.* New York: Carol Publishing Group, 1996.

Wagner, Laurie, and Anne Hamersky. *Expectations: Thirty Women Talk about Becoming a Mother.* San Francisco: Chronicle Books, 1998.

ABOUT THE AUTHOR

When Michelle Brenner and her husband, Mark, decided to have their first baby, Michelle was in for a dramatic change in her life. She went from having an active career to managing pacifiers and Pampers.

During her pregnancy, Michelle began looking for a concise yet comprehensive guide to help her prepare for the transition to parenthood. When she couldn't find one that met her needs, she wrote one herself—with the help of Dr. Carole Buchholz, a certified pediatrician and mother of two.

Michelle uses her experience in management training and communications to help guide new moms and dads through pregnancy and the first few months at home with their baby.

Michelle lives with her husband and two children, Paige and Samuel, in Santa Barbara, California.

ACKNOWLEDGMENTS

Writing this book has been an amazing process (my husband would say, "an amazingly long process!"). In fact, it's been both. Over the years, there have been countless people ranging from babysitters to strangers on planes who have passed along words of wisdom and encouragement. To each one of you, a heartfelt thanks!

To my dear friend, Nella, thank you for believing that "I could."

To "the girls," Elisa, Cathy, Nancy, Laura and all the mothers of young children who participated in focus groups and with questionnaires, your insights and experience give this book its resonance.

To my kind and gentle book shepherd, Gail. In my wildest dreams I couldn't have hoped for a better editor. You taught a speaker to write and helped birth a beautiful new book. Thank you, dear friend.

To Chris, Barbara and Peri, your technical skills are nothing short of fine art! Thank you for sharing your gifts with me and investing them in *Here Comes Baby!*

Kristi, I count the hours you spent on the layout and cover development as a labor of love. Thank you for being a part of my dream.

To the superb medical team that brought my children safely into this world, thank you for your hand in these miracles.

To my dear family and friends, your support and encouragement along the way are why this book got finished! Thank you for joining me on the adventure.

My humble gratitude to God for the grace, mercy and courage to live each new day that you give me.

Quick Order Form

E-mail orders: msbrenner@yahoo.com

Telephone orders: Call 805-687-2606

Postal Orders: Samuel Paige Group
1124 Estrella Drive
Santa Barbara, California 93110

I would like to order _____ copies of *Here Comes Baby!* @ $12.95 each.
(For quantity discounts and special sales please call 805-687-2606.)

Name: _____

Address: _____

City: _____ State: _____ Zip: _____

Telephone: _____

E-mail address: _____

Sales tax: Please add 7.50% for books shipped to
California addresses.

Shipping by air: U.S.: $4.00 for the first book and $2.00 for
each additional book.

International: $9.00 for the first book and $5.00 for each
additional book (estimate).

Make checks and money orders payable to: Michelle S. Brenner

THANK YOU FOR YOUR ORDER!